THE HOME
I WORKED
TO MAKE

THE HOME
I WORKED
TO MAKE

VOICES FROM THE
NEW SYRIAN DIASPORA

Wendy Pearlman

Liveright Publishing Corporation

A Division of W. W. Norton & Company
Independent Publishers Since 1923

This is a work of nonfiction.
Individual names have been altered in certain cases.

Copyright © 2024 by Wendy Pearlman

For information about permission to reproduce selections from this book,
write to Permissions, Liveright Publishing Corporation, a division of
W. W. Norton & Company, Inc., 500 Fifth Avenue, New York, NY 10110

For information about special discounts for bulk purchases, please contact
W. W. Norton Special Sales at specialsales@wwnorton.com or 800-233-4830

Manufacturing by Lakeside Book Company
Book design by Brooke Koven
Production manager: Louise Mattarelliano

ISBN 978-1-324-09223-0

Liveright Publishing Corporation, 500 Fifth Avenue, New York, N.Y. 10110
www.wwnorton.com

W. W. Norton & Company Ltd., 15 Carlisle Street, London W1D 3BS

1 2 3 4 5 6 7 8 9 0

To the Syrian and Palestinian families who taught me about home
by welcoming me into theirs

Contents

THE HOME
I WORKED
TO MAKE

Kareem

UNNAMED LOCATION

In my life, there are three faces that I will never forget.

One was the face of a father I met after his son died of cancer. That was the face that made me want to study medicine.

The other was my own father's face after they arrested my brothers.

And then there was the face of Mohammed's mother when we learned that he had been killed.

I WAS in high school when the revolution began in 2011. Tunisia and then Egypt were all over the news. I would light up when I watched. We saw that people had voices and that their voices could be heard. I had always had a general sense that we were not living free lives. Then, all of a sudden, it became possible to stand up. Most people thought there was no way that something like that could happen in Syria. But a Syrian Revolution page began on Facebook and it called for a protest on March 15. My friends and I counted down: twenty days left, fifteen days left, ten days, five.

March 15 came, and I got ready for the demonstration. People were saying to bring Pepsi to combat the tear gas. I packed four cans in my backpack and pretended that I was going to school. My parents caught me and refused to let me leave the house. Like most Syrians, they were terrified that their children would get hurt.

There was another demonstration three days later, and I went. Prayers concluded in the mosque and people started chanting for freedom. I built up the courage to join, but then managed to escape when security agents charged in and started beating people. The feeling of protesting was something out of this world. It was like someone who had lived his whole life without an achievement and then did something remarkable. Or like someone who spent six years in medical school and finally got his degree.

☙

I MET Mohammed when we started medical school together in October 2011. I was the youngest of my siblings, and he was the eldest of his. He was someone who could handle responsibility. I trusted him with any problem. He was the one I sought out for advice. We were not close before we started going to demonstrations, but protesting together cemented our relationship. There is no bond like sharing that experience. We would go to school in the morning, attend lectures, and then go out and protest. Mohammed became my brother. Not a cousin or a friend, but a brother.

It was my job to make signs. I would buy four sheets of A4 paper, tape them together, and fold them again and again until they were tiny enough to hide in my pocket. When we got to the demonstration, I would unfold the sign to its full size. I did not want to write just any slogan. I wanted to write something that inspired thought. One of my slogans became really popular: "Bitter is the taste of freedom in the mouth of slaves."

☙

WE WERE eight hundred students in our first year of medical school. We slowly became divided between those who supported the regime and those who did not. After a while, separation became tension, and tension became hatred. Your political position became your identity. You couldn't trust anyone. When you spoke with someone, your safety depended on knowing if you could trust that person or not. Knowing if this person is with the regime or opposition was not just a question of fact. It was a necessity.

Once in chemistry lab, a regime supporter came and pounded me on the back. He accused me of putting a chemical liquid on another regime supporter. I told him that this liquid was for a particular assignment that I hadn't even started yet. But there was nothing I could do to defend myself against him. At any point, he could report me to the Students' Union.*

The Students' Union was a group of students, but they had power to function like a branch of the secret police inside the university. And they saw that people were getting bolder. Mohammed and I started going to demonstrations every day. Other students were posting signs criticizing the regime or writing on desks and walls. Once there was even a protest on campus, though that was really risky. Some students formed what they called the "Union of Free Syrian Students." It was like an alternative to the official Students' Union, ready to replace it when the regime fell.

The Students' Union decided that they needed to put a stop to this. They arrested a graduate student in the faculty of dentistry. Later, we got news that he died under torture. The Free Students' Union posted something on Facebook about him. I copied the post and pasted it on my own page. A friend sent me a Facebook message urging me to delete it, as those words were dangerous. But I had used my privacy settings to share it only with friends I trusted, so I was not afraid.

---

* The National Union of Syrian Students, founded when the Baath Party seized power in Syria in 1963, has long served as the ruling party's arm of surveillance, control, and repression inside Syrian universities. Along with the Revolutionary Youth Union based in middle and high schools and the Baath Vanguards Organization targeting elementary schools, the Students' Union has served as part of the apparatus through which the regime seeks to embed its rule throughout society. After 2011, the Students' Union was accused of assisting in the torture, disappearance, and murder of thousands of university students suspected of opposing the Assad regime.

FIRST SEMESTER exams came. The Students' Union knew that all students would be present on campus, and this was a chance to grab whomever they wished. One of our friends was taking an exam when Students' Union members marched into the lecture hall. They walked directly to him and took him away.

The following week there was another exam. I got on the bus to go to the university but couldn't shake my feeling of unease. I thought about my friend who was arrested and about the student killed under torture. I decided not to go to campus.

I got off the bus and walked around, passing the time until I figured the exam was over. Then I called Mohammed to see how it went. He answered, but with none of his normal friendliness. There was no "Hello" or "How are you?" Just "Where are you?" His voice was cold and rough. I replied that I was on my way to him. But I knew that something was wrong. I kept walking and then it occurred to me: he was trying to tell me something. The tone of his voice was communicating the opposite of his words. He was telling me: "Stay away. Stay as far away as you can." He was telling me, "They are here. Don't come."

I MADE more calls and heard the rest from another friend. The Students' Union had arrested Mohammed. They were with him outside the library, waiting for me to come.

That was how I learned that I was wanted. I went to an Internet café and deactivated my Facebook account. I felt like all eyes were on me. I felt like every person passing on the street was coming to arrest me. Later I got a call from an unfamiliar number. I guessed that it was someone from the Students' Union and I didn't answer.

The next week they arrested more students, including other friends. The rest of us realized that they were coming for us, one by one.

Mohammed's whereabouts remained unknown, but others who were arrested were eventually released. I spoke with them and slowly pieced together clues. The Students' Union arrested the guy who had once messaged me on Facebook about my post. When they interrogated him, they opened his account and saw his message to me saying "Delete this." From there, they entered my page and saw my reposting from the Free Students' Union. They also interrogated another arrested student, demanding to know who was in the Free Students' Union. When he said that he didn't know, the head of the Students' Union brought him a sheet of paper and pen. He commanded him to write my name.

I WENT to Mohammed's family after he was arrested. His mother was in such a state . . . I don't have the words to describe it. I continued to call and visit them after that. His mother knew that I was Mohammed's closest friend. When she looked at me, she seemed to see him.

Weeks passed without any news about Mohammed. His family paid tens of thousands of dollars to try to learn anything they could about where he was and how he was doing. Different people promised that they would bring information in exchange for payment, but they were all lying.

Three months went by before they finally got a call. A man who had been in prison with Mohammed was released. He told them that Mohammed had undergone terrible torture. He was at his side when Mohammed died from his injuries.

I got the news and went immediately to Mohammed's mother. Her grief was unlike anything I'd ever witnessed. She kept crying, "Mohammed is gone. Mohammed is gone." As I said, in my whole life there are three faces I will never forget. Hers is one of them.

No one ever came to my house to arrest me. I was only wanted at the university. In the 1980s, universities in Syria were a center of political activity. The government knew this and didn't want it to be repeated. They wanted universities to provide zero space for opposition. They wanted universities to be silent except for a single voice: the voice of the regime.

The Students' Union understood that if one person got killed, everyone else would learn the lesson. They needed a sacrificial lamb, and Mohammed was that lamb. I might have been one too. And that's why I never set foot on campus again.

I tried to move on with life, but no longer saw a future. All of these questions never left me. Why should I be banned from learning? Why should I be denied my chance to become a doctor? Because I wrote something on Facebook? I started having nightmares. Every week I had at least five, and some nights I had many. They always built on the same idea: somebody was chasing me, and I was running to escape. I would wake in a panic. A few seconds would pass before I remembered: I am a wanted person. I am still being chased and am still trying to escape. The panic would linger. The feeling I lived with during the day was no different than the feeling I had in my dreams.

☉

I stayed in Syria for another year and a half. It became a society of war and abuse. There was no place for people who simply wanted to breathe, who wanted a more open life. A society during war exists for those who know how to take advantage of war conditions for their own profit. Those are the people who win. When you live in a society at war, it changes you from the inside. It changed me too. It's not just the course of my life that changed. My personality and my soul also changed.

The morning I left Syria, I took the bus to the cell phone company to discontinue my number. The bus was packed, so I stood near the door. People kept coming on and off, on and off. A soldier in uniform came on, and I stepped off the bus to make room for him. He got on and motioned at me to get back in. I stood on the sidewalk for a moment. He repeated, "Come back inside."

I looked at him and asked myself: Is this going to be my last image of Syria? A man carrying a weapon? I thought, I will leave you more than this spot on the bus. I will leave you all of Syria. I am leaving, and I leave this entire jungle to you.

Introduction

THE NEW DIASPORA

S ince coming to power in 1970, the regimes of Hafez al-Assad and his son Bashar have ruled Syria through violence, co-optation, and fear. In 2011, against the backdrop of the Arab Spring, millions of Syrians took to the streets in the hope of replacing single-party authoritarian rule with a new government based on freedom and accountability. As the government responded with ferocious repression, revolution morphed into a multisided war that killed hundreds of thousands, plunged the country into ruin, and forced more than half the population to flee. Of Syria's pre-war population of about 21 million, approximately 5.5 million people have become refugees in the Middle East, 1.5 million have received asylum in Europe, 368,000 have been resettled elsewhere, and 7.2 million have been internally displaced.[1]

Commentators have analyzed the Syrian war through lenses such as protest, violence, geopolitics, sectarianism, extremism, and refugee crisis. Fewer have considered what Syrians' extraordinary experiences can teach us about something so commonplace that it touches every human life: home. Every person has some understanding of home, whether positive or negative, straightforward or complex, present or absent. In literature, television, film, and music, home is a beloved trope. Generations of Americans, for example, were captivated by how the Ingalls family built a house on the prairie, how E.T. struggled to find its way back to home in outer space, and how Dorothy realized the true meaning of home after her wanderings through Oz. TV sitcoms

bring us into the intimate home spaces of fictional families whose fur-
nishings and décor become as familiar as our own. Popular songs pay
tribute to home's sweetness and the longing that carries people miles
and miles to reach it. Across languages and cultures, expressions such
as "Welcome home" and "Make yourself at home" are among the most
tender well-wishes to offer or receive. Variations on the term "homeland" are a staple in political rhetoric and in government agencies such
as the US Department of Homeland Security, connecting the emotional weight of home to matters of policy and sometimes invoking
home as justification for state violence.

Across these varied domains, references to home are ubiquitous
because the idea of home strikes at the core of what it means to exist
as a person in the world. The experience of being *denied* home is no
less central. Across millennia, crises ranging from political upheaval
to ecological collapse and nuclear disaster have compelled people to
flee their homes. From the exoduses of ancient times to the population
movements of the Second World War, forced migration has shaped the
societies that refugees leave behind, the new ones into which they settle, and the world at large.

At the time of this writing, more people are displaced globally than
ever before. Nearly a third of them, the single largest group from any
country, are from Syria. The scope and speed with which Syrians became
refugees, as well as the diversity of places where they now find themselves, is staggering. The impact of displacement is all the more dramatic
given that, before the war, Syrians typically remained in the communities in which they were born—and often in which their parents and
grandparents were born—unless compelled to move for studies or lack
of job opportunities. War thus did more than uproot millions of people.
It also uprooted millions who might otherwise never have left the towns
or neighborhoods to which they had strong, multigenerational bonds.

All of this makes the new Syrian diaspora an especially powerful
context in which to ask: What is home? Is home a place, a feeling, or
people? Is it embodied in the objects that one would most want to save,
if forced to choose among them? Or is it constituted by nonmaterial
moments and memories? How is home lost, and can it be rebuilt? What

if it never really existed to begin with? Do we need something to call home, or can we find contentment without it? These are questions of universal import, and Syrian refugees, migrants, and asylum-seekers have garnered uncommon insight into them. Even before leaving Syria, many witnessed their hometowns become nightmares of bombardment, siege, and death. Some communities transformed beyond recognition as houses were flattened, streets destroyed, and entire cities emptied of family, friends, and neighbors. Now scattered near and far, displaced Syrians are tasked with rebuilding their lives and livelihoods in countries where they might never have imagined stepping foot. For many of them, the word "home" has thus come to connote twin challenges: first, the challenge of creating a new home in a foreign place; and second, the challenge of mourning the loss of an old home and making sense of the horrific circumstances in which it became lost.

This book explores the varied meanings of home through testimonies from thirty-eight displaced Syrians now on five continents. It does not purport to tell their stories as completed journeys. Rather, it brings together a series of moments in which individuals reflect upon journeys that remain ongoing. Each personal narrative is its own meditation on leaving home, losing home, seeking home, finding home, or not finding home. Across the collection of narratives, a new concept of home emerges: Home, for those who do not have the privilege of taking it for granted, is both a struggle and an achievement. Before creating a home in the world, people must define home for themselves. Determining what home means demands discovering who one is and how one finds peace. It entails realizing what matters most and what one ultimately can do without. This is a kind of awareness that does not come without adversity, soul-searching, or even pain. Home, in other words, takes work. And when people arrive at something that they feel is home, it is the home they worked to make.

Displaced persons' lives and self-reflections have much to teach everyone about home. The violent dislodging of persons from their established moorings, and their labor to establish themselves anew, can reveal fundamental truths about belonging and attachment that are obscured in more settled circumstances. Viewing refugees in this light—as bearers of special wisdom on the question of home—presents a new perspective on forced migration. It exposes the hollowness of discourses that portray refugees as powerless victims or accuse them of exploiting tax-funded services in host states. No less, it lays bare the problem of tokenizing the successes of migrant doctors, entrepreneurs, or star pupils who defy the odds to earn accolades. Instead, it insists that simply developing a feeling of home is *itself* a feat that defies the odds. This understanding of home encourages appreciation for all the work that refugees and migrants do to find home, as well as empathy for those who are still searching. And it calls upon everyone, everywhere, to learn from what they have to say.

☉

THIS UNDERSTANDING of home as struggle and achievement diverges from common understandings of home primarily as a place. In everyday language, people often refer to home as something physical, material, and locatable. It is a house, neighborhood, town, or country. It is where we grew up, live, or return when need arises.

Equating home with a place, however, is not so simple. It invokes major debates about the processes through which people transform abstract, amorphous "space" into "place" when they define its bounds and believe in its value. A traditional strain in scholarship on these matters views human communities as inherently connected to specific geographies. Similar ideas undergird the international political order today. Nation-states that guard their sovereignty, and nationalist movements that sometimes challenge them, embody the conviction that peoples have distinct territorial homelands and the right to govern themselves on that soil.

Yet not everyone embraces the notion of an organic connection linking people to particular lands. Some theorists propose that territorial homelands are not a truth of human nature as much as a social fiction developed to justify nationalist structures of political power. Moreover, some insist, globalization and technology have blurred borders, making modern life increasingly transnational and de-territorialized. In this view, people today can choose to make, unmake, or remake home anywhere. They may claim multiple homes simultaneously or live happily without any home at all.

Whether organically rooted or liberated from all roots, home is not simply a spatial entity. It is also a temporal one. One might feel "at home" somewhere right away. To claim something as home, however, usually requires some passage of time. The accumulation of experiences, memories, and daily routines is what eventually converts a strange environment into a familiar and even precious one. Furthermore, an important part of identifying something as home is often the experience of leaving and then returning, a dynamic that lies in connecting points in time as much as it does in contrasting points in space. Still, while continuity of time can be a constituent element of home, home itself is rarely continuous. What one identifies as home often changes over the course of one's life, as do the reasons for identifying it as such. If you were to ask yourself at different junctures of your life what home means to you, you might be surprised at how your answers differ, and how each answer provides a window into who you were at that stage.

Beyond time and space, home is also a feeling. For some, the defining emotional experience of home is a sense of security. In that understanding, home is the haven where we find protection from the dangers of the public sphere and reprieve from its stresses. For children, home can offer a sanctuary from angry neighbors, bad days at school, or an unexpected fight with a friend. In adulthood, home may represent a break from a nine-to-five job, the value of which has taken on new dimensions as remote work becomes more commonplace. During the twilight of life, some people move to residences and rehabilitation centers that replicate home environments of comfort and care, while others enlist different forms of support to "stay at home" despite the challenges of aging.

Home may thus seem one and the same as security—except that homes can also be unsecure. Haunted houses and horror movies that center themes of home invasion are captivating and terrifying because they take the idealized safety associated with home and invert it. In the real world, homes that are sites of substance abuse can be places of unpredictable rage. For those subjected to domestic violence, home might be synonymous with pain. Refugees offer another lens on dangerous homes. Legally defined as persons unable or unwilling to return to their country of origin owing to a well-founded fear of persecution, refugees are often colloquially described as people "forced to flee home." But when a home becomes so violent that it forces one to flee, is it still home? Can one long for a place even when it exposed them to lethal threat? Refugees' experiences encourage us to think critically about whether security is a necessary component of home, and what home means when security is absent.

Others argue that the essence of home is not security, but love. Stitched on pillows and emblazoned on doormats, the idiom "Home is where the heart is" suggests that home is not necessarily where one resides, but wherever one's loved ones are. How, then, do people make homes without the people who are dearest to them? Forced migration brings this question to the fore. Some refugees are utterly alone when they take flight. Even those who flee with companions typically leave behind the bulk of the relationships that once comprised their social worlds. While voluntarily leaving a familial home can be a valued step toward independence, being ripped from it against one's will is traumatic. This is all the more true in social contexts such as those in Syria, where extended families once lived in close proximity and visited each other regularly. Young people typically remained in their parents' homes until they married. Some neighborhoods were nearly entirely constituted of relatives. Today, by contrast, hardly any Syrian family is intact. Parents, children, siblings, cousins, and others are scattered across continents, and some have not seen each other in years. Where is home when one's heart is in many places? Can forging new loves make a home out of a foreign land? Displaced peoples' journeys reveal the different ways that home and heart can coincide, and how people experience home when they do not.

Another perspective identifies home with neither security nor love, but authenticity. To be at home is to be who one really is. For some, home is the private retreat where one escapes from public pressures and, alone at last, does not have to put on appearances. For others, it might be the social environment where they are drawn out of their shells by the people who accept them unconditionally. Whatever circumstances facilitate it, this understanding of home as letting down one's guard, like other understandings, contains the seeds of its opposite. For some adolescents who identify as gay, lesbian, queer, nonbinary, transgender, or gender-nonconforming, a childhood home might be precisely where they are compelled to hide their true selves. Under those conditions, it might not be home, but rather leaving home, that enables one to live authentically. Does this mean that the familial home was never home at all? Or can someone value something as home even if one is not genuinely "at home" there? These questions are pertinent for some migrants and refugees who find themselves in alien environments where it is difficult to be themselves. Newcomers might feel that they must give up some part of their identities to live in a new place—or, conversely, that they must give up some part of living in a new place to preserve their identities. Finding home and finding authenticity may thus seem incompatible, at least at first.

A final understanding of home shifts emphasis from authenticity to aspirations. Several theorists advance this view, locating home in the striving and the fulfillment that it uniquely enables. In this spirit, anthropologist Ghassan Hage, a scholar of diasporas and himself an immigrant from Lebanon to Australia, defines home as a place of possibility.[2] In contrast to those who visualize home as a shelter, he describes it as a mother's lap where we temporarily rest before we spring into action again. Fellow anthropologist Michael Jackson concurs that home is a place made meaningful because "what we do has some effect and what we say carries some weight."[3] Jackson spent years among a nomadic aboriginal people, exploring what home signifies for communities who do not dwell in fixed locations. He discovered that, for them, home is defined by personal growth and strong connections between the individual, the collective, and larger geographical surroundings.

If home is fundamentally a base from which to actualize one's purpose in the world, then many live under circumstances that deny them prospects for home even when they have places to call their own. Oppressive political systems can leave polities terrorized by repression, tormented by corruption, and demeaned by everyday abuses of power.

Entrenched inequality can lock communities in generational cycles of poverty, and structural racism can subjugate people based on their color or ethnicity. Under these and other conditions, individuals' homelands might suffocate their ambitions rather than encourage them. When places of origin deny justice and opportunity, some people rebel, some take flight, and some make do. Others take it upon themselves to carve out intimate mental or physical spaces where they experience the fulfillment that their external environments thwart. It is in this sense that cultural theorist bell hooks calls attention to how Black women create nurturing "homeplaces" where their loved ones recover from the weariness of daily struggles, restore their humanity, and ultimately make lives that feel "worth living."[4] For hooks, building a home of care is itself an act of political resistance.

Ultimately, what makes home special is that it touches all these components: place, time, security, love, authenticity, fulfillment, and still other social and emotional experiences that give meaning to human life. For many of us, these elements fuse so effortlessly in a single home that we hardly perceive them as being distinct. Cultural geographer Yi-Fu Tuan argues that this is the essence of rootedness.[5] In Tuan's view, one is completely at home when one does not even think about whether or not one is at home—one just is. To be rooted, in his words, is to be unreflectively secure and comfortable in a particular locality.

That is what makes the perspectives of the unrooted so valuable. Refugees do not have the luxury of being unreflective about home. On the contrary, being forced from home can bring them to contemplate home in freshly discerning ways. And one of the many things that these contemplations reveal is what happens when the various dimensions associated with home do *not* converge. Quests for security and love go in different directions when people leave a place due to profound danger while their family and friends remain there. The longing for fulfillment and for authenticity become disconnected when one yearns for the habitual comfort of a native land, but that land does not provide possibilities for achievement. Under such circumstances, people face difficult choices about what they most need in a home and what they must relinquish. They might try to stitch together distinct aspects of home, create some elements from scratch, or make peace with a home with permanent cracks or holes. The resulting home might not feel complete, but its reconstruction will bear the dignity of both struggle and achievement.

(◎)

HOME IS thus multifaceted and multidimensional. If a single word embodies its opposite, however, it might be "exile": the punitive removal of a person from a homeland. Celebrated writings on exile are often saturated with nostalgia, painting wistful portraits of homes left behind and articulating an insatiable yearning to be reunited with them. One of the most famous expressions of these sentiments comes from Edward Said, a Palestinian American intellectual compelled to spend most of his life far from his birthplace of Jerusalem. Even as he built an acclaimed career in the United States, Said described exile as "like death but without death's ultimate mercy." Exile, he wrote, is "the unhealable rift forced between a human being and a native place, between the self and its true home: its essential sadness can never be surmounted. . . . [T]rue exile is a condition of terminal loss."[6]

Such ideas about the agony of exile are not limited to literary essays. They also form the basis of common assumptions about what refugees seek. Syrians in places from Egypt to Norway have told me that the most persistent question they hear even from well-meaning locals is, "Do you want to go back home?" The question has an innocuous premise: exile is arduous, home is the country left behind, and refugees' natural desire is to return. This might be true for some who flee war, persecution, and dictatorship. Yet it does not hold for all. Some Syrians say that Syria was never a true home, and life there was itself a kind of exile. They describe how citizens were alienated from each other due to the ways that omnipresent security forces and pervasive undercover informants infused social relations with a hazy air of distrust. They recall a sense of estrangement from their true selves insofar as they had to conceal their real opinions and instead chirp false praise for the president. Even those proud of their Syrian heritage could thus feel exiled inside a country that the government claimed as "Assad's Syria," and that killed citizens who dared to claim it as their own.

What is home and what is exile when the place of one's birth represents not only "the nourishment of tradition," in Said's words, but also degradation and violence? Such is the dilemma for millions of displaced Syrians today. Looking back to the towns and villages that they left behind, many Syrians articulate cherished recollections of childhood innocence, familial wholeness, cultural familiarity, and communities where no one was a stranger. Yet they also express unblinking realism about the injustice and violence that transpired on that soil. For the millions who supported the 2011 uprising, forced migration has deprived them of not only their physical homeland, but also the dream of creating a new homeland that could offer freedom and protect basic rights. For these children of the revolution, geographic dislocation is not necessarily the beginning of exile as much as another stage in an arduous search for a true home.

The complex interconnections between home and exile often disappear in anti-refugee rhetoric in refugee-hosting states. There, a common demand is simply that refugees "go home." In Lebanon, the second-largest host of Syrian refugees, a doctor famously took to the airwaves to blame refugees for rising rates of cancer. A federation of trade unions proclaimed a "National Campaign to Liberate Lebanon from the Syrian Demographic Occupation" and, in 2022, the government announced a plan to repatriate 15,000 Syrian refugees per month. In Turkey, the largest host of Syrian refugees, it is not uncommon to find locals who believe that their government gives Syrians free housing, pays their phone bills, or waives university admission exams on their behalf—ideas that Syrians themselves know to be laughable. With recent polls indicating that more than 80 percent of Turks favor deportation,[7] Turkish elections have become contests in which candidates battle to be the most anti-refugee. In the 2023 presidential runoff election, for example, the opposition candidate grossly inflated the number of Syrian refugees in Turkey, promised to deport millions immediately, and posted signs declaring "Syrians will go!" When the incumbent president won the election, he pledged to deport one million refugees.

Hostility to Syrian refugees has also sometimes run high in European countries. There, too, the language of "home" surfaces explicitly or implicitly as justification. "Let's not forget, the Syrian who comes to us has still his Syria," a leader of the Alternative for Germany party declared in 2015, "but if we lose our Germany, then we have no more home." A few years later, billboards cropped up at bus stops in Germany, emblazoned with an aerial view of a Middle Eastern cityscape and the Syrian flag. Speaking directly to refugees, the signs declared in German and Arabic, "The war is over, Syria needs you." The Danish government, alleging that Syria is safe for repatriation, revoked residency permits from nearly a hundred Syrian asylum-seekers in 2020, instructing them to return to Syria or be held indefinitely in deportation centers. As a member of Parliament supportive of the policy declared in a social media post addressed to Syrians: "Denmark is not your home."

Syrian refugees' own opinions about going "back home" point to a strong consensus: most refugees will only return to Syria if it is safe and most do not believe that it is safe or will become safe anytime soon. A 2023 survey of Syrian refugees in the Middle East conducted by the United Nations High Commissioner for Refugees (UNHCR) found that about 25 percent of respondents hoped to return to Syria within five years and another 40 percent hoped to return "someday."[8] When asked if they intended to return within the next year, however, only 1 percent said yes. These respondents did not eschew return because they were finding comfort and ease in exile; indeed, 90 percent indicated that, in refuge, they lacked the income to cover their basic needs.

Official public statistics on deportations remain elusive, in part because international law prohibits repatriating individuals to places where their lives or liberty are in danger. However, human rights groups estimate that several tens of thousands of Syrians have been forcibly returned from Turkey, Lebanon, and Jordan. In addition, UNHCR estimates that about 7 percent of officially registered refugees have voluntarily returned to Syria.[9] Human rights investigators who have interviewed refugees who chose to go back to Syria report that they live in fear and suffer from a dire lack of basic services like water, electricity, and healthcare. Many have faced abuses such as arbitrary detention, torture, and forced disappearance; most regret their decision and would consider leaving Syria again if they could.[10]

These figures and findings lay bare the dilemma of home under conditions of oppression inside Syria and threat of expulsion outside of it—at times on top of extreme economic deprivation in both. Displaced persons who are barely surviving in exile might not want to return to their country of origin, while those barely surviving in Syria might long to leave. For those stuck between an unlivable "here" and "there," home might not exist in either location. It is all the more remarkable that some continue to strive for something to call home, nonetheless.

☙

I LAUNCHED this project during the 2011 Arab Spring. Proficient in Arabic and having studied the Middle East for more than half my life, I was captivated by the joyous street demonstrations, inspiring shows of solidarity, and jaw-dropping courage of the millions who risked their lives to demand freedom. I decided to collect personal stories from Syria, where a history of brutal state repression made mass protest especially astonishing. Since it would be dangerous to conduct interviews inside Syria, I began to interview Syrians who had fled their country.

I started my first research trip with a few names that, as days became weeks and then years, snowballed beyond what I had ever imagined. I moved from one interviewee to another by becoming a world-class pest: I asked everyone I could if they knew someone from Syria who might be willing to share their story with me. *Everyone.* Friends, neighbors, colleagues. Friends and family of friends, neighbors, and colleagues. People I met at parties or events. People with whom I had studied Arabic fifteen years prior. People with whom I connected on social media. I ended interviews by asking interviewees if, now having a sense of what an interview entailed, they knew others who might be interested in doing an interview too.

Sometimes my asking yielded no new connections. Sometimes it introduced me to awe-inspiring people I never would have met otherwise. Once, an interviewee posted about my project on Facebook, inviting any Syrians interested in talking about their journeys to contact me. For the next few days, my phone lit up with queries from people on several continents asking to make an appointment. Several of their testimonies now appear within these covers. As I delivered public lectures, visited classrooms, and published writing based on interviews that I conducted, including pieces translated into Arabic, I gained new credibility in Syrian circles. Now, it is not unusual for people to approach me after I finish a talk and offer to do an interview or check with a friend who might. Seeing what became of their stories seemed to make people more eager to share them.

Along the way, I have done all I can to insist that no one feel under pressure or expectation to speak with me. I seek to interview only those who genuinely want to be interviewed. Often, the people who sit with me to record their stories remark that they had not previously wanted to talk about their lives, but now felt the desire or even need to do so. As I see it, my task is to be in the right place at the right time to intersect with people who are, on their own, arriving at that feeling. In sustaining this work over many years and building networks across many countries, I have been fortunate that this has happened repeatedly.

Since I began this project, I have conducted interviews with more than five hundred Syrians of different ages, genders, ethnicities, religions, hometowns, and socioeconomic backgrounds. I have spoken with people who left Syria under different conditions and at different points in time. In addition to doing interviews in the United States, I have made interview trips to Jordan (2012, 2013); Turkey (2013, 2015, 2016, 2018, 2020); Lebanon (2016, 2018); the United Arab Emirates (2016); Germany (2016, 2017, 2018, 2021, 2022); Sweden (2016, 2017); Denmark (2016); the United Kingdom (2018); and Norway (2018, 2022). As videoconferencing became commonplace during the COVID-19 pandemic, I began conducting interviews remotely, as well. This allowed me to reach Syrians in still other countries, such as Australia, Brazil, Canada, Chile, the Czech Republic, France, Georgia, India, Japan, the Netherlands, South Africa, and Sudan.

Through the years, I have spent countless hours getting to know displaced Syrians by staying over as a houseguest, volunteering at schools and shelters, attending concerts and art exhibits, and chatting in coffee shops. Between 2016 and 2022, I spent five summers in Germany, traveling extensively throughout the country and undertaking an immersive dive into the large Syrian community in Berlin. In 2018, in a town on the Turkish-Syrian border later ravaged by the February 2023 earthquakes, I taught a weeklong workshop on oral history to Syrian refugee teens with the aim of empowering them to do their own interviewing projects. These and other ways of being with people—listening, observing, eating together, building relationships, and doing what anthropologists sometimes call "deep hanging out"—allowed me to experience, with all my senses, different facets of home-making across a new diaspora. It exposed me to new trends in familial and gender roles; in how people dress, carry themselves, and arrange their living spaces; and in how refugees and locals interact with each other in stores, transport, and other public spaces. As I bore witness to the same kinds of challenges, tensions, and triumphs that my interviewees described, I gained assurance that what I recorded in one-on-one interviews reflected patterns relevant to much larger populations.

Completing interviews was one part of this project. The next step was working with them in writing. I recruited assistants to help transcribe audio-recorded interviews and, in many cases, simultaneously translate speech from Arabic to English. A single interview transcript could run up to 25,000 words, or about one-fourth the length of this entire book. Transcripts bore the free, circuitous flow of informal conversation, with many tributaries. To transform speech into text, I had to cut, condense, and often rearrange the sequencing of people's narratives, as well as edit for readability.

In 2017, I used interviews that I had collected to that date to write *We Crossed a Bridge and It Trembled: Voices from Syria*. A curation of testimonial fragments chronicling the evolution of the Syrian uprising and war, *We Crossed a Bridge* begins with the backdrop of Syria's pre-2011 authoritarian status quo and concludes with the exodus of millions of refugees. Although that book ended there, the Syrian story did not.

The Home I Worked to Make takes Syria's refugee outflow as its point of departure. Featuring a completely new cast of speakers, all interviewed after *We Crossed a Bridge* was published, this book explores what has become of those who fled war and now pursue new futures around the world.

During the rapid-fire early years of the Syrian uprising, my interviewees expressed an urgent need to document what was happening. I did too, and that was the motivation behind my first book of Syrian testimonials. As years passed and the pace of events in Syria slowed, however, a different need became palpable: the need to make sense of it all. The frequency and ferocity of military battles decreased, but other battles, such as the struggle to extract meaning from loss and find oneself amidst a shattered world, gained force. These are battles that receive too little attention. Public interest in wars is typically strongest during their shocking outset or their particularly horrific peaks. Then interest wanes. What we miss in this short span are the ways in which the "aftermath" of crises—if there ever really is an "after"—are no less important than the height of crises. The impact of war lies not only in scorched earth and casualty counts, but also in how violence transforms the people who endure it, with ripple effects that alter entire societies. Such changes are not always immediately apparent, either to observers or to survivors themselves. They are revealed with time and reflection.

IN RECORDING Syrians' reflections, I did not set out to write a book about home. I typically begin interviews with a single prompt: "Tell me about yourself." Interviewees respond by narrating their lives however they wish, and I follow the train of that narration. And again and again, I found that the train passed through ideas about home. As I noticed the theme emerging organically and recurrently, I began to ask about it directly. My mention of the topic was often met with a knowing nod, smiling eye, or response along the lines of, "I've been thinking a lot about that myself lately." In asking about home, I sensed that

I was not starting a conversation, but requesting permission to enter conversations that many Syrians were already having with each other or within themselves.

Here it is important to note that Arabic does not have an exact equivalent of the English "home." Rather, it offers a range of words that each capture one of the many dimensions and experiences of what English-speakers call home. In Arabic, *watan* translates to "homeland." It expresses connection to a native land, often with heavy connotations of collective nostalgia, national identity, and political loyalty. Indeed, the Syrian Army features *watan* in its slogan: "Homeland, Honor, Devotion." *Balad*, or "country"—often modified to refer to "my country," "our country," or "the country"—carries some of the emotional weight of homeland, but without its political undertones. Moving from the national to the domestic, *bayt, manzil*, and *dar* are closer to "house." Those terms convey the private and familial intimacy that *watan* and *balad* do not, but in everyday practice tend to be synonymous with a physical residence more than some larger social or psychological anchor. *Intima'* means "belonging" in the sense of descending from, being connected to, or having membership in. Not inherently related to place, *intima'* taps into abstract attachments that are felt but not necessarily situated geographically. Importantly, the word derives from the linguistic root نمى (n-m-a), meaning "to grow" or "to increase," and thus carries hints of personal development.

I listened for these and other expressions as people shared their stories with me and recruited all of these words in asking speakers what home meant to them. That home invited so many different words further emphasized its quilted character as a composite of many elements. No less, it cultivated my interest in how displacement can sever elements that once fit together, casting them in a new light and generating new awareness about them. Still, as I moved the concept of home to the center of my work, I also became attentive to circumstances under which it either did not emerge or did not seem to resonate. This was most starkly the case when I met with Syrian refugee families who were struggling to find money for their next meal or rent payment, who could not access healthcare that they desperately needed, or who were consumed by worry about loved ones facing various forms of urgent threat. When I met with such families in Jordan, Turkey, and Lebanon, for example, my queries about home sometimes elicited inquisitive stares more than deep musings. This also taught me an important lesson. Abstract questions about the meaning of home, it seemed, might be a luxury that one can afford only after more fundamental material and security needs are met.

Back in my own home in Chicago, I deepened my understanding of home by reading from cross-disciplinary academic literatures. I continued to ask whomever I could, "What does home mean to you?" I talked to people who had moved a lot or never at all; people who were very close to the families in which they had grown up or who spoke to them rarely; people who had created new families of their own or who lived alone; people who invested heavily in the domestic spaces in which they lived or hardly cared about their surroundings. I found that some people had ready definitions of home and others struggled to put it into words. For nearly everyone, however, "home" was a word that opened a pathway to thinking about who they were and what they valued. I came to appreciate how home is a meeting point where people with remarkably different life stories can communicate with each other. Even people who can scarcely imagine each other's worlds find the question of home meaningful. And that makes it a unique vehicle for fostering human exchange and empathy.

⊚

THE CORE work of this project consisted of doing and transcribing interviews and subsequently condensing, editing, and arranging testimonies as text. In addition, there was one final and crucial step in the process of seeing this book to its final form: seeking interviewees' approval of their narratives prior to publication. I thus returned to speakers and asked if they were content with the editing of their interview, if they wished to make any changes, and, given their current circumstances, if they preferred to use their real name or a pseudonym. Getting back in touch with interviewees entailed more than one hundred messages across multiple platforms. In some cases, it required that I enlist the help of mutual acquaintances, who reached across the world to help me find someone whose contact information had changed.

The process of obtaining approvals proved important not only ethically but also emotionally and intellectually. For many interviewees, reading their testimonies after the passage of years or even months was a moving experience. Several told me that they smiled, cried, or were struck by how their outlooks had changed. A few had moved countries or continents yet again, undergoing second or third exiles that were kinder or harsher than the exile I had documented. They engaged with their testimonials through the lens of those new experiences.

These conversations taught me a lot about the temporal and contextual aspects of home. Temporally, they revealed how a single interview captures only one snapshot of a person's continually evolving understanding of home. The narratives in this book do not recount the entirety of any life experience, but rather how individuals make sense of life at some particular moment. Contextually, renewed communication with interviewees confirmed how legal, political, and economic circumstances shape prospects for home-making. In host countries that offer rights, assistance, and opportunities for education and employment, many people who had initially experienced estrangement were, slowly but surely, building a sense of belonging. Where the status of refugees remained precarious, by contrast, initial feelings of home rarely withstood the weight of insecurities that compounded year after year. Still, persistent hardships do not mean that those individuals will not arrive at a feeling of home sometime in the future. Their stories have not ended yet.

THE NARRATIVES that follow, and the concept of home as struggle and achievement that emerges across them, make several contributions. Most broadly, they create points of human connection. These are stories of diverse human experience, and readers can engage with their many layers depending on wherever they find themselves in their own life journeys. These stories may especially speak to anyone who has ever migrated, descends from people who have migrated, or loves someone who has migrated and wants to learn about their life between worlds. Readers with such backgrounds can examine where their ideas about home converge with or diverge from those of the speakers in this book. Readers who have not had close interactions with refugees and migrants, or are not sure how to ask refugee and migrant acquaintances about their lives, might find that these narratives offer a starting point. Beyond migration, there is much in these stories that will resonate with anyone who has ever felt out of place, undergone a big move, or carefully considered what they need to feel settled in time and space. Regardless of one's relationship to home, these stories can inspire deeper thinking about what belonging means and how different forms of belonging make each of us the people we are.

This book also aims to push public and scholarly conversations on displacement in new ways. First, it shifts discourse from "refugee crisis" to diaspora-making. In 2015, an unprecedented 1.3 million refugees and migrants arrived in Europe. What some called Europe's "long summer of migration" became linked with images such as those of overloaded dinghies marooned in the Mediterranean, crowds marching across Europe, and, most hauntingly, a young boy's lifeless body washed up on a Turkish beach. Displaced peoples' lives since then have been more difficult to capture. They comprise moments in which people piece together greetings in new languages, memorize unfamiliar streets, applaud children at graduation ceremonies, await fateful bureaucratic decisions, or hunt for places to buy foods that taste like their memories. This book foregrounds these everyday challenges and victories, as quiet as they are formative. These are the lived details through which people work to make something called home, long after stories of dramatic arrivals fade from public view.

Second, most narratives of diaspora-making take on a specific population in a specific location. By contrast, the testimonies in this book are global in scope. They introduce us to cities and countries where large new Syrian communities are putting down strong roots, to places where communities are perilously insecure, and to where isolated individuals forge paths largely alone. Stories from these and many other locales show the folly of referring to diasporas as if they are unitary entities, such as "the Armenians," "the Vietnamese," or "the Irish." In delving into the experiences of Syrians as individuals, this book shows that these communities are far from homogenous. The people who speak to us in the pages that follow all come from a single country that is only about the size of the US state of Washington. While they come together as members of a new Syrian diaspora, each has a unique experience of home.

Third, most accounts of diasporas are written long after they become established. The narratives to follow, however, document how diasporas form in real time. Speakers describe a transitional phase of home-making that bridges their pre- and post-exilic lives. Once a diaspora becomes rooted, it can be easy to forget the myriad trials and triumphs that brought that rootedness into being. Snapshots from the process of diaspora-making capture these details. The decades to come will see continued generations of Syrian Germans, Syrian Turks, Syrian Canadians, and more. They will forever impact the countries in which their parents and grandparents settled, even as their absence from Syria also transforms Syria. Tomorrow's diasporans can use this book as one of many resources with which to build their own ideas of home.

Finally, these stories spotlight what refugees can teach nonrefugees about their own cultures, societies, and selves. As Yi-Fu Tuan reminds us, the unrooted may reflect on their surroundings in ways the rooted often do not. Newcomers identify assumptions and ponder habits that locals sometimes hardly notice, no less interrogate. Refugees' observations thus not only yield understandings about their own extraordinary lives; they also offer a fresh perspective on every country in which they settle.

ORGANIZED IN seven parts, this book roughly follows the chronological arc of displacement journeys, beginning with departures from a country of origin and passing through different experiences en route to or within countries of settlement. While this sequential structure upholds home as a process unfolding in time, it does not intend to imply that home-making is bound to a predetermined teleology. It can be tempting for countries receiving refugees to see them as traveling from despair to deliverance. This does not happen for all displaced persons, nor ought it be assumed that it should. Not all people begin and end in the same spot or traverse the same fixed and predictable stages. In some of the testimonies that follow, speakers transition from losing old homes to gaining new ones. In others, speakers do not feel like they had a home to begin with, do not build a new home, or do not feel that they need one. If there is any linearity in this book, it is due not to redemption or happy endings but to the weight of time. That people recount the stories of their lives as arriving at some semblance of normalcy suggests a deep human desire for stability. This may demonstrate a tremendous capacity to adapt or perhaps a determination to remain in the familiarity of the past. Either way, narrations testify to how people find meaning, even under the cruelest circumstances.

To best showcase a diversity of experiences of home, some interviewees appear in only one of the book's seven parts, whereas others speak to us repeatedly. Each part begins with a short introduction in which I briefly reflect on that section's main theme, provide some context for issues to be discussed, and preview the speakers to come. These interludes in my voice also aim to assist readers in recognizing speakers from prior parts and following the thread of their journeys. Readers interested in tracking specific individuals can refer to the table of contents and follow the installments in their story. Alternatively, readers can approach testimonies like solos in an ensemble choir—appreciating the uniqueness of each voice as it weaves in and out of song, while also sitting back to be moved by the power of the collective. For readers interested in more background on the political context of speakers' experiences, a timeline at the end of the book presents key dates in Syria's modern history and especially the course of conflict and refugee flight since 2011.

Taken together, these narratives are a tribute to the new Syrian diaspora, showing how and why their stories matter for the world as they do for Syria. Across the globe, people hear about Syrian refugees on the news, see them in passing, or know them as coworkers, classmates, friends, or neighbors. Yet even when locals develop relationships with these newcomers, they may feel that they grasp only the surface of their stories, as the deeper realms of their experiences remain inaccessible due to language barriers or other kinds of distance. I hope this book is one entryway into what becomes a continued process of learning about the diversity and complexity of paths to and from forced migration.

I also hope that these stories offer lessons. To those who oppose allowing refugees and migrants into their countries, these voices offer a sample of the real people on the other side of erected walls. To locals in communities where refugees settle, these narratives demonstrate the immense power of even the smallest acts of kindness and solidarity. They remind us that everyone has a choice about whether to greet strangers with generosity or neglect, or with openness or hatred—and those choices can change lives. To those involved in designing or implementing migration, asylum, and resettlement programs, these stories are a glimpse into the inner worlds of the diverse individuals that those programs aim to serve. In particular, they offer newcomers' perspectives on "integration," one of the most prominent notions in public and policy discussions on refugees today. In voicing refugees' needs, challenges, frustrations, and aspirations, the speakers in this book suggest that integration is not simply a matter of language acquisition or financial self-sufficiency. Nor ought it demand that newcomers abandon their identities or culture. Rather, integration is a dynamic two-way process in which both migrants and the host society change and adapt. For many refugees, integration is also the process through which they make peace with a painful past, attain conditions that respect their dignity in the present, and grasp prospects for a future where they might not have to think so much about whether or not they belong. This behind-the-scenes emotional labor is rarely visible, but it is central to the hard work of home-making in and after displacement.

Most importantly, I hope that the stories that follow, and readers' willingness to learn from them, send a message to refugees around the world: Whether or not you have found something that you call home, you are not alone.

—Wendy Pearlman
May 2024

I

LEAVING

SARA M., NOUR, GHANI, FATIMA, GHADA, MASRI, OKBA, MAHA, HANI, ALAA

Refugees' lives do not begin when they cross an international border. Neither do their complex relationships to home. A deeper exploration ought not start when refugees arrive, but instead address how and why they leave.

While some Syrian refugees have escaped ISIS or other rebel groups, the overwhelming majority have fled violence perpetrated by the Assad regime. Some flee to escape the military service that is compulsory for all young men. Others flee to evade being imprisoned for their activism or for reasons as arbitrary as being related to a wanted person or coming from a particular town associated with the opposition. Political detention in Syria has long been synonymous with torture, starvation, disease, and captivity in underground cells so overcrowded that detainees take turns sitting and standing. To be arrested is to be condemned to a slow and painful death, while loved ones are condemned to the torment of indefinite uncertainty and hope that the disappeared person might emerge alive someday. Individuals who fear that their arrest is imminent often try to leave the country rather than risk that fate.

Others have fled the violence of war. The Syrian Army's shelling and aerial bombardment of areas under rebel control—often deliberately targeting civilian neighborhoods, hospitals, schools, and bakeries—have been the chief military driver of refugee flight. The army has also conducted "starve or surrender" campaigns during which it blocked entry of food, medicine, and other essentials to the communities that it besieged. These and other strategies have aimed to punish and demoralize those who rise up against the regime, making daily life impossible until people either submit to Assad or leave. Significant violence in the Syrian war has also been committed by non-Syrian actors. This includes bombing by the Russian Air Force, on-the-ground fighters from Iran and the Lebanese group Hezbollah, incursions and occupation by the Turkish Army, strikes by Israel, and attacks by militants from around the world who joined ISIS or other extremist groups. Such external interventions not only intensify the suffering that pushes out civilians but can also undermine their very sense of Syria as a home. The power of other parties in and over Syria suggests that the country is no longer a single, sovereign nation-state belonging to its people. Rather, there are now many Syrias divided among outsiders.

Not all who escape Syria are impelled by physical violence. Economic catastrophe has also undone this once middle-class country, driving away those who have the means to leave. Since 2011, the Syrian pound has lost 99.6 percent of its value.[1] Some 90 percent of Syrians currently live below the poverty line and 60 percent lack sufficient and reliable access to food.[2] Many areas have access to water and electricity for only minutes a day, if at all. Bread is rationed, public transport is increasingly unaffordable, and fuel for heating can be all but impossible to find. And even in this grinding economic misery, other dangers and degradations—from stifling government corruption to the specter of military conscription and predatory warlords—remain acute.

Syrians' stories of leaving home unfold against this merciless backdrop. Yet these stories also carry traces of the liberation, joy, and camaraderie that many experienced in the revolution. The uprising was a struggle both to overthrow dictatorship and to transform a nominal homeland that served a privileged few into a true homeland that belonged to all. For many, the revolution itself became that homeland insofar as its champions gave voice to their own aspirations, cultivated once unimaginable solidarities with others, and uncovered a new attachment to Syria as a place worthy of the greatest sacrifices.

The narratives to follow explore these themes. Sara M. describes her experience in the revolution and how, upon learning that she is wanted for interrogation, she attempts to escape. Ghani and Alaa are arbitrarily arrested by government forces; while they are among the lucky ones to make it out of prison, renewed threats convince them to leave before it is too late. It is the brutality of bombardment and siege that drives Fatima, Ghada, and Masri from their homes, hometowns, and ultimately their homeland. For Hani and Maha, mandatory military service is the impetus for flight; when a conscript defects rather than fights on behalf of Assad rule, he—and maybe his whole family—must hide from punishment or flee. In Nour's experience, it is family members who impose the decision to leave despite her pleas to remain. For Okba, chance dictates this decision when he travels abroad temporarily and finds himself unable to go back.

These narratives remind us that Syrian refugees often become internally displaced inside their country, sometimes repeatedly, before they eventually depart. Those who leave are those who can afford transport, sometimes smugglers, and usually bribes along the way. They risk arrest at checkpoints and gunfire from border guards, especially after the overburdened countries neighboring Syria shut their doors to refugees. In offering a window into these and other conditions of leaving, the narratives that follow also point to the complex ways in which homelands do or do not offer what people need from home. Displaced persons' final memories of their first homes, and the events through which they become past homes, imbue who they are, what they seek, and what belonging means to them. They are essential frames of reference that refugees and migrants carry into home-making in countries of settlement.

Sara M.

Someone told me that there was going to be a demonstration that Friday in Salamiyah. Before going out, I paused on the doorstep and asked myself, "Are you ready to bear the consequences or not?" I was enormously afraid, but I said to myself, "Whatever will be, will be."

You put yourself on the side of your people. You're standing up for yourself because you're part of those people. When people rise up against power, right is always on their side. It doesn't matter if we're good people or bad people. We're humans and we should have rights. Every Syrian family has been harmed in some way by this regime. Every Syrian knows someone in prison. All of us have suffered from broken dreams. All of us had jobs or were deprived of jobs because of corruption. Our memories are filled with oppression and government repression.

I got to the protest an hour early and saw people beginning to stand in a circle. There was a group of women I didn't know. They asked me, "Are you with us or against us?" I said, "I'm with you." We held each other's hands and started walking down the street.

The feeling was something out of this world. Young people were crying of happiness. Before that, you felt broken. You were always saying, "Yes." This was the first time you said, "No." That first demonstration was the most beautiful event of my life. It was like the day I was born. People gave the most beautiful thing they had to give during those first six months. They helped each other. They cleansed themselves of all the rot that the regime had transmitted. It was extraordinary.

◎

WE STARTED printing and distributing statements. We'd meet and discuss political issues every day. These were the first steps of people getting to know each other. For safety, I took on a new revolutionary name: Sara. My real name, Rasha, was forgotten. My personal identity became Sara, the political activist. Sara suits me more than Rasha. Now I don't know if I can express myself any other way.

In the fifth month, I met someone named Abu Tarek. He'd been a political prisoner for ten years in the 1980s. Abu Tarek asked me to do a different kind of work. Secret work. He needed someone who didn't have any problems with the security forces and could move freely between governorates. In particular, he needed someone female.

He asked, "Can you go to Damascus whenever you want?"

I said, "Yes, of course. I can move freely."

The truth was that I couldn't. I had my job and my family. But I made a decision. I was going to do any work related to the revolution, and nothing was going to stop me.

He said, "Can you travel with me to Damascus?"

I replied, "Any time."

Abu Tarek knew somebody who was donating money for injured people and families who had lost children. I would be the one to deliver that money. The regime wouldn't expect that someone from a religious minority was working with the revolution.* They wouldn't suspect a

---

* The population of Syria is majority Sunni Arab Muslim, with smaller Christian, Druze, Jewish, Shi'i, Ismaili, and Alawite religious communities, as well as distinct Turkmen, Armenian, Circassian, and Kurdish ethnic communities. While most of modern Syria has been distinguished by coexistence, communal differences have also become entwined with politics in complicated ways. The Assad family and most high-ranking military officials are from the Alawite minority, estimated to comprise about 11 percent of the population. Consistent with its own minority roots and Baath nationalist ideology, the Assad regime has long presented itself as a protector of religious minorities. Since 2011, one

thing of a young woman who wasn't wearing a hijab. In the eyes of the regime, delivering aid was one of the most dangerous things you could do. This was especially the case if you are from a religious minority because you're ruining the regime's entire narrative that it is the one protecting minorities from terrorism.

That's how it began. The next day I woke up, Abu Tarek called me, and I left. We went to Damascus and came back.

We were very careful. We'd sew money inside a sweater and deliver it to activists. Once I stuffed money inside a cookie. Activists never asked each other about their real names. Of course, we were terrified all the time, but we never had any trouble because secrecy kept us safe. I was living with my sister at the time, and not even she or her family knew why I was going to Damascus. Abu Tarek's wife didn't know either. Abu Tarek was very careful because he didn't want to be imprisoned again. In prison, they had beaten one of his legs until it became so disfigured that it was two centimeters shorter than the other leg. He didn't like to talk about the torture. He just said, "Detention is like death, but worse."

⟨◎⟩

A GROUP of us activists created a political body called "The National Collective in Syria." There were members from different provinces across the country. Every day we discussed what we wanted in Syria. We'd discuss things like secularism, Islamism, and the meaning of freedom. Our goal was to show that Syrians can work together. We aren't just people belonging to different religions or ethnic groups. We're not a majority and minorities. We are a political people and we have political rights. And to get our political rights, we are fighting this regime.

It was a very dynamic time, like a river just carrying us away. Things

---

of its strategies has been to rally the loyalty of minorities by portraying the popular uprising as an extremist Islamist and sectarian threat to Syria's secular multicultural character.

were going very well until one man who was helping us became wanted by the security forces. He had to leave Syria. Then the regime decided to target Abu Tarek. Salamiyah was a small town, and Abu Tarek was a recognizable face. He was hiding in different houses but could be captured at any moment.

We stayed that way for some months and then decided to move to Damascus. The situation was different in a big city. I rented a house for Abu Tarek in my name. My mission was to provide cover for a wanted person.

Abu Tarek and I became like Siamese twins. We shared the same Facebook and Skype accounts. We had the same daily dialogues and discussions. We thought along the same lines. I'd wake up in the morning and read all the news related to the situation in Syria. Then, I'd tell Abu Tarek about everything I read. After that, we would do our rounds across Damascus. We became so attached to each other that no one knew Abu Tarek without knowing Sara or knew Sara without knowing Abu Tarek.

WE HAD to move houses five times because landlords became suspicious of what we were doing. Still, I never had any security problems. And then one day my family called and said that the State Security Service had come asking about me. I was wanted for interrogation.

We slowed the pace of work and started having fewer meetings. Then the Air Force Security Service arrested one of the women to whom we had given assistance. They tortured her. One of our contacts got access to her interrogation file. It showed that they were asking her two questions: Who is this Sara who brings the money? And to whom is she distributing money?

That was it. Abu Tarek and I were the only ones who knew everything: money, names, other information. And I was the one documenting files on the computer. If I got detained, it wasn't just me who would be gone. The whole group would be gone.

A decision was made that I should leave. I would go first to Lebanon. Activists in our group tried to get information to make sure that my name wasn't on a wanted list at the border. I packed my luggage and said goodbye to Abu Tarek. That was supposed to be the final goodbye. I took a taxi to the border and, there, an officer asked me to get out of the car. By coincidence, he was from Salamiyah. He should have arrested me, but he didn't. Instead, he took me to a room and said, "Look, you're wanted for interrogation. Here's some advice: pay some money and have someone close your file." And then he let me return to Damascus.

I called Abu Tarek and said, "Boss, I'm on my way back."

He said, "Where are you?"

"I'm coming back."

"Stop kidding. Did you get to the border?"

"I'm not kidding. Make breakfast, I'm coming back."

Nour

LATAKIA, SYRIA

We lived in a family neighborhood. My aunt was a neighbor and two of my best friends lived in the opposite building. My grandparents were one block away. When I think about the happy memories of my childhood, they're all at my grandparents' house. Our tradition was for the family to gather every Thursday night. Everyone had to be there, no excuses. It was when all the grandkids sat and talked with Grandpa. I remember these conversations so well.

In sixth grade, you take Syrian nationalism classes for the first time. The whole class is basically about how amazing the president is and how doomed we would be without him and his family. We had only one source of history. They controlled what kind of books could enter Syria and what kind of websites you could visit.

But Grandpa had seen a lot of history personally. He said, "Don't believe everything they tell you in school. Those are lies. But keep this talk between you and me; you cannot tell anyone." I remember thinking, "Maybe Grandpa is remembering things wrong." I asked my mom. She told me about the Hama massacre and about a friend of hers who was detained for fifteen years without charges.* When Mom spoke,

---

* Against a backdrop of accumulating popular grievances and civic agitation in the late 1970s, a breakaway faction of the Muslim Brotherhood, Syria's strongest opposition movement at the time, began a campaign of attacks against the Assad regime. The regime retaliated against the Brotherhood, spurring the

she was so scared. She said, "Don't talk about this anywhere outside our home. It can get us all in trouble." That's how I learned that what Grandpa said was true.

Grandpa and Mom were the main figures in my life when I was growing up. They both had compassion for helping others. They emphasized that we should never feel that we are better than anyone else. People in need would come to our house and talk to Grandpa or Mom, and they would help them out. I knew that I had all this privilege so that I could help. And that was the reason why I had to leave Syria.

⟨⊙⟩

I WAS in my third year at Tishreen University studying architecture. One of my classmates was kidnapped by other students who supported the government and was brought to a security branch office to be interrogated. He was from a city known for opposing the government and the regime considered everyone from there to be traitors.

I knew that he could get really hurt or die in detention because he had no connections to powerful people who could get him out. I decided to go to the dean. I asked, "Please, could you help release him? Students are upset. We'd like to arrange a silent protest in front of the rector's office." Later that day, when I came back home, I got a phone call from my dad's friend, who worked in a high position in the Ministry of Education. He'd heard about what happened and told me that, from now on, I should call him to take care of things. The next day, the arrested student was released. He had bruises from being tortured.

That semester, there were some demonstrations on campus with the flag representing the Syrian opposition. I wasn't involved in any pro-

---

group's radicalization and 1982 insurrection in the town of Hama. The regime responded with a twenty-seven-day scorched-earth assault that flattened entire neighborhoods and indiscriminately killed an estimated 20,000–40,000 people, many of them civilians with no political involvement. It subsequently became taboo, or cause for government suspicion, to speak about the incident.

test. Around December, my dad's friend, the high-ranking administrator, called him and asked him to bring me to his office. We went.

The administrator asked me, "Nour, what did you do?"

I said, "I don't know what you're talking about. I didn't do anything."

He said, "You can be honest with me. What did you do at the university?"

I said, "Really. I didn't do anything."

He showed me a paper and said, "They have a report on you and now you're wanted for interrogation." I was being linked to what was happening at the university, even though I hadn't participated in anything. I wish I had, to be honest. At least then the accusation would be true.

I told him, "Honestly, I didn't do anything."

He said, "Well, they don't care. With what's written on this paper, they'll still interrogate you."

The minister turned to my dad. He said, "You're here because we're friends. I think that you should leave the country."

My dad was really angry. I had sabotaged things for my whole family. My dad, my mom, and my brother were not safe anymore. I said again, "Really, I didn't do anything." But it didn't matter at that point. I pleaded, "I'm sorry, let's stay. I swear I won't do anything. I swear I'll be good."

֎

I WENT back to the university. One day, two guys came for me. Imagine you're eating breakfast in the cafeteria, and two guys sit down right in front of you and stare. One was wearing military clothes. I was really scared.

I stayed there until the lunch break and finally left for the bathroom, just as a way of making sure that they were really there for me. When I got up, they followed me. Then I knew I needed to get out of there. I blended into the crowds in the hallway and managed to get out of the building. I got in my car and saw them behind me, getting in another car. I felt so much panic that I cried. I honestly have no idea how I got home. Our house had an electric gate; when I got inside it, they were locked on the outside. I went in the house, and they stood there and watched.

THAT WAS our last night in Syria. I didn't want to leave. I cried and fought to stay. But my dad knew what was best for us. He said, "No discussion. Just pack."

My parents said that we would be leaving for only a month or maybe six months. A year maximum, and then we'd be back. I only packed some winter clothes. My dad told me not to tell anyone that we were leaving, so I didn't say goodbye to people. But Grandpa and Grandma were a huge part of me. I couldn't leave without saying goodbye to them.

They always woke up super early, so I snuck out of the house around 4:30 a.m. Those men could have still been waiting outside to arrest me, but I didn't care. When I got to Grandpa and Grandma's house, they were having their morning coffee. Grandpa was feeding the birds on the staircase. He saw me coming and said, "Nour, what are you doing here so early?"

I said, "I came to see you. I need to say goodbye."

Grandma understood. She was sad and angry at the same time. She said, "Don't listen to your dad. We can take care of things. It'll be fine."

But I think Grandpa understood. Deep down, he knew that there was something wrong and that I might have done something that made it dangerous for me to stay. I remember him saying, "Don't listen to Grandma, just leave. Study. Work on yourself. It's a different world out there. Don't be scared."

Grandpa was proud. Grandpa was wise. I was blessed that I got to spend my childhood with him. I feel like we never said goodbye properly—if that's even a thing. The year after we left, he was diagnosed with cancer. He died a year after that.

Ghani

DAMASCUS, SYRIA

I left school when I was sixteen years old. My sisters and I had to find work so we could support each other, and especially our sister with special needs.

I used to comb my sisters' hair and fix it in silly ways. I dreamed of being a beautician and doing makeup and hair. I started working for a barber. I worked without pay for six months, just so I could learn. Then I rented my own little shop in a working-class area. We saved money and bought a barber shop. Life got better.

The revolution started. I didn't take any part in it. I kept away from politics because I had my family to look after. Our neighborhood wasn't safe, so we moved to a different area and, after that, to another area. One day in 2012, I was working in my shop. Someone from the army came and arrested me and the customers too. They accused everyone in the shop of being an armed group.

For thirty-five days I didn't see the sun. The cell was four or five meters. We were one hundred and sixteen people, all without clothes. The youngest was thirteen years old, and the oldest was eighty-two. We didn't have a toilet. Instead, we used a little corner near where we ate. I didn't have a name. I was number 13/9.

One of my friends was tortured with electricity. I saw people who got the drill. Then one day the interrogator said to me, "You're next."

I said, "I'll do anything you ask, just don't take me to that room. If you ask me if I put Jesus on the cross, I'll say that I did it. Whatever you say, I did it. Just don't take me to that room."

I stamped my finger on four completely blank sheets of paper. The interrogator wrote that I created a group and was planning an explosion or something. They sent me to court. The judge looked at me and said, "I can tell from your face that you're not an extremist." She told me, "I'm going to put your file in my drawer, but I can't keep it more than one month. You have one month to leave the country."

I went back home. I'd lost nearly twelve kilograms. I had a long beard, long hair, yellow skin. My mom didn't know who I was until I spoke. When I looked in the mirror, I didn't know myself. For a time, I couldn't walk at all.

After a few days, I started to get better. People came and visited to welcome me back. One person was from the intelligence services. He told me, "You're a barber. If we're looking for someone and he comes to get a haircut, just send us a text." He wanted me to work as an eye for the government. I couldn't say no because they knew where I was. I agreed but told him that it was impossible now because I was still not well. He said, "Okay, I'll give you a few days."

That's when I decided to leave the country. It was a miracle I got out. My name was at the checkpoints, but I paid money and got through.

Fatima

Our building was in a strategic place between Freedom Square and a cemetery. On one side, people demonstrated every Friday. On the other side, they'd bury whoever got killed. Our apartment was on the fourth floor. I'd stand on the balcony and watch the demonstrations. I wanted to participate, but my mother told me that I couldn't do anything that would put the rest of the family at risk. I never marched in a single protest. But from above, I tossed flowers onto funerals so they might land on the martyrs who were killed during demonstrations and whose bodies were carried on people's shoulders. I felt that I was participating in some way.

The state increased its level of violence little by little. First, they used tear gas, then batons, then bullets. During Ramadan, we'd wait to sundown to break the fast and then, suddenly, the shelling would begin. I remember once the shooting went on for four hours. I thought that no one would be left alive in our town. My nephew was only two years old, but he'd go sit by a column in the house because he understood that was the safest place.

Going through war numbs your feelings. When the army withdrew after one of the massacres, we saw residents rolling dead bodies in white shrouds like they were wrap sandwiches. Once we were on the balcony when a van carrying corpses passed by. We looked and said, "Oh, corpses," and then continued drinking our coffee. The shelling was so constant that people had to hurry to bury people. They couldn't

46

close up the graves completely, and we'd smell the stench of death. We were all living in one giant graveyard.

When they began bombing from airplanes, we were driven out of our home for the first time. When we got back, we found glass shattered and the refrigerator wrecked. The electricity was almost always cut during those days. Some strawberries had spoiled and looked like a pool of blood. The walls were riddled with bullets. I said, "Our house has been stamped with a special revolutionary tattoo."

We had to leave home again many times after that. Sometimes we left for a week or ten days. Each time I'd plead with my mother to let us go back. At first, we moved to a lower floor because it was safer when they bombed from airplanes. But then they began bombing cars on the street, and nowhere was safe anymore.

Our whole family gathered: my grandmother, uncles, everyone. Everyone was at the end of their nerves. At any moment we could all die. We thought, "If they raided us right now, how are we going to defend ourselves?"

Still, I never imagined that we'd really leave. My room was where my calm was. Staying there was everything to me. My sister was in love with our neighbor, so she didn't want to leave either.

Ghada

ZABADANI, SYRIA

When the first women protested in Zabadani, I was scared and didn't say a thing. But I'd wished that I'd joined them. I told myself that, next time, I would. I helped gather a group of thirteen women. We didn't know each other but we became friends after the first demonstration. We called ourselves "The Revolutionary Women of Zabadani." I was painting signs, writing banners, and sewing flags. Visitors were always coming to my house. My husband was a farmer and didn't care much about politics. He used to say, "I'm a farmer. If the regime falls, I will remain a farmer. And if the regime stays, I will remain a farmer."

The army started doing night raids. The Imam would use the mosque PA system to warn people. As a code, he'd say, "Be careful with the frost on the roads." Later the army executed him. The army would barge into people's homes in the middle of the night and yell, "Get up! Where are the armed groups?" Men lost their minds when they saw the army raiding their bedrooms, with women still in their pajamas. I'd sleep in my coat and hijab.

Men started saying: To stop a weapon you need another weapon, not a flower. As women, we tried to keep demonstrations peaceful. Men didn't listen. I stopped going to demonstrations when they became about men showing off their weapons and firing randomly in the air. Weapons have to be used ethically, at the right time and in the right way. Weapons gave the army a reason to shoot at us.

The regime started shelling Zabadani from the surrounding mountains and then it bombed with barrel bombs.* They set up checkpoints around the city and inside it. Our town became a militarized zone, and people started to flee. I told my husband, "I can't stay here any longer, I'm scared for the kids." I took our five children and went to Damascus. My husband stayed back to work the farm.

Two months went by, and I wasn't able to see him. It was a very difficult time. I was alone and exhausted. My husband and I were texting all the time. He wanted me to stay in Damascus where it was safer but sensed that I was upset. One day he texted me saying, "Come back to Zabadani, it will be the best decision you make. When you come, I'll have a surprise for you."

That morning we loaded our things in a van to go back to Zabadani. My husband had slept at the farm that night. His nephew and his wife were there too. They heard gunfire. Apparently, rebels shot at a truck that was delivering food to the army. There was a big villa nearby, and the shooting gave the army an excuse to enter the villa and loot the entire place. I think that those soldiers and officers wanted cover for their theft, so they reported that they found weapons in the villa. And then they came to our farm. The nephew's wife later told me that the army opened fire before they entered. My husband was still sleeping in his underwear.

My husband and his nephew were arrested around nine o'clock that morning. I arrived at 11:15 and heard what had happened. I started to search. I went to the State Intelligence office. They told me that my husband had been transferred to Damascus. I went to Damascus and started circling the intelligence building. I remembered from the Quran when Jacob searched for Joseph. I started yelling my husband's name like a crazy person. "Tarek! Tarek!" The guard laughed at me and told me to go away.

---

* "Barrel bombs" are a kind of improvised munition used by the Syrian regime, typically oil drums, gas tanks, or other containers packed with explosives and shrapnel. First used in 2012, barrel bombs have been dropped on civilian areas, indiscriminately destroying homes, medical facilities, schools, and bakeries. Barrel bombs became the war's most devastating source of death, destruction, and refugee flight, with human rights groups estimating that the regime had dropped nearly 82,000 barrel bombs by spring 2021.

I kept going to different areas to ask people about Tarek. I paid so many bribes to try to get any information, but to no end. Once, someone in Qudsaya who had been released from prison wrote something on Facebook, including a list of people with whom he had been in prison. Tarek's name was on the list. I asked the Facebook Page Admin to put me in touch with that person. I wanted to travel to Qudsaya, but I'd get arrested at the checkpoints because I was on the list of wanted people. I decided to do a "reconciliation" with the regime. Basically, you get a document that says, "After realizing the truth of the conspiracy against us, I have decided to return to the embrace of the homeland." At the top it says, "type of weapon," meaning the weapon that you were caught possessing. You sign your name and get it stamped.

With the reconciliation document, I travelled to Qudsaya and met the person who had listed the names on Facebook. He was very sick and thin as a skeleton. I showed him my husband's photo and he immediately recognized him. He said, "We spent a year and a half together in prison. I was released and maybe your husband will be released too."

I waited, but nothing happened. I couldn't control myself. Anytime I heard anything related to Tarek I had to do something. I kept asking people and kept hearing tragedies. In prison, the guards would throw yogurt on the ground, and detainees ate it off the floor. Somebody told me how three detainees had to share a single piece of bread. He said that once two people were so hungry that they told the guards that the third person had cursed the president. That person was taken away and executed, and the two detainees ate the bread.

☉

THERE WAS a cease-fire between the regime and rebel groups, but it collapsed. Later that year, Hezbollah entered the area.* That's when it became too dangerous to stay. I took my kids and moved to Lebanon.

---

* In 2011, Hezbollah—a Lebanese political party and armed group that emerged to fight Israel's 1982 occupation of South Lebanon—joined its backer Iran in intervening militarily in Syria on behalf of the Assad regime.

We planned to stay a month until the campaign ended. But things got worse and worse. There were checkpoints all over and they were arresting everyone on the wanted lists. My reconciliation document wasn't going to work anymore.

Zabadani and other areas nearby came under siege. They became one big grave. My siblings and friends who were still there began to starve. My sister once sent me a video of when the local council tried to distribute tiny pieces of chocolate to children. It became very chaotic, with kids stepping on each other to get a piece. I still remember the shout of one child in particular: "Please! I'm hungry!"

Masri

AL-QUSAYR, SYRIA

When the army raided al-Qusayr for the first time, thousands of soldiers surrounded the town and blocked the main roads. They said they were searching for armed men. At that point, very few people even had hunting rifles. But the soldiers believed that everyone in town was armed. They searched door to door, entering like a SWAT force, ready to shoot.

I realized that I was going to be arrested. My family started crying and saying, "Farewell, we'll never see you again." I rushed to my bedroom, which was in the far back of the house, almost in the yard. I waited and thought, "Oh God, I'm done for." The soldiers came and searched all the rooms but, for some reason, didn't come to that room. They called all males to bring their IDs and go into the street. I just waited. And then they left.

After that, I escaped for a few months and stayed in a village near Aleppo. When the army started arresting people there too, I decided to go back to my town. I thought, "If it's risky here and risky back there, at least I should be in my place."

◎

WHEN I got back to al-Qusayr, my family had already left for Damascus, which was safer. The first thing I wanted to do was go home. A front line had opened between the army and the rebels, and my family house was on that line. People said, "You can never go there again. It's not safe."

Where else could I go? I had no Plan B, so I tried to make it back home. An older relative took me by the hand. One of the rebels became our guide. At some points, we crawled so snipers couldn't see us. We walked from one house to another through holes in the walls and eventually made it.

Our house had been bombed and there were so many holes in the walls and the ceiling. Most of our stuff had been stolen. The house was not simply dangerous; it was uninhabitable. I'm not sure how I felt at that point. I don't really know if it felt like home. Furniture is replaceable. Damage of houses and buildings was something that we saw every day. That didn't mean a lot to me. Maybe when I saw the ceiling, that hurt.

I left and never came back.

⊙

IN AL-QUSAYR, I started teaching in a school basement. I felt that my presence was meaningful. Parents said that school was safer for their kids than staying home because most houses didn't have basements. And after months of not going to school, kids needed something normal.

All I owned was a backpack and a laptop. I'd take them with me and stay with friends. After a week or two, I'd think that I'd stayed too long, so I'd call another friend and stay with him. Because I spoke English and had some IT skills, people would ask me for help translating a message or doing things related to the Internet. In exchange, people would let me stay with them or take a shower or have lunch or dinner.

Most of the time, I stayed with a friend who had defected from the army. Another friend who'd left the army stayed there too. We stayed in one room of the house and wouldn't go to the other rooms because they faced a checkpoint and could get hit by mortars. Then another friend had a situation similar to mine: he went to his home and to his relatives' homes, and none were livable. He joined us and we became a group of four. The friend who owned the house said, "Now we've got two pairs to play cards."

When that house was also bombed, each of us found his own alternative. One joined a rebel group. Another went to live with his aunt. I went to the house of another friend and then to another and then another. I kept moving from place to place. No door in my town was locked during that time. If there was shelling or any bombs dropping from the sky, you could open the door to any house and hide inside. Guys would leave their motorcycles unlocked in case something happened and you needed to grab one and get away. People shared food, shared diesel. Everyone volunteered to help each other.

The most terrifying thing during those days was the warplanes. Once I saw a warplane and lost two friends on the spot. But at some point, you no longer care about being killed. You become very sarcastic. They start bombing, and you say, "The music has begun." People can adapt to any circumstances—it's part of our survival skills as humans. The most difficult thing is waiting for what happens next. Facing death becomes easier than waiting for it.

⊙

I STAYED in al-Qusayr until Hezbollah's final attack. It was very fierce. When Hezbollah started controlling the area, some civilian groups decided to evacuate the town. The evacuation took three days. We walked to the area of Qalamun in the Damascus countryside. There was no food, no water, no medicine, nothing. Some people attacked each other for a sip of water. We walked only at night because it was too dangerous to walk in the daylight. People carried the wounded on their shoulders. Helicopters were in the sky, shooting randomly at everyone. We lost three hundred people along the way.

When we finally reached Qalamun, we were five thousand zombies. We were very hungry, very thirsty, very tired, and very lost. We'd been sleeping on rocks for three days and had mud on our faces. When we got there, I saw two journalists, one Italian and one Belgian. They'd been kidnapped by some group that eventually joined ISIS. I knew the Italian was a foreigner because he was wearing white pants. White pants?! Without anyone noticing, I talked to him and got his name. Later, I sent like a million emails to Italy on his behalf. I wrote police stations and police departments. I was risking my life doing that, and it's one of the things that I'm very proud of.

ⓒ

I SETTLED in Qalamun, which was hosting tens of thousands of people who had been fleeing other towns during the past two years. Several of my relatives were already there. They'd invite me for meals, which is how I survived the first months.

During those visits I became close to one relative whom I'd gotten to know a few months before we left our city. We fell in love and got engaged. When you survive death, hard decisions like marriage become simple: Life is short, let's not waste any time.

I found a job as a communications officer at a field hospital. Meanwhile, I started posting on Facebook about the case of the foreign journalists. Two members of the group that had kidnapped them attacked the field hospital; they wanted to kill me for damaging their reputation. Later they apprehended my cousin, who shares my exact first and last name. They were about to break his fingers when they realized that he wasn't me.

I didn't want my story to end by getting killed by a rebel group. I was ready to sacrifice my life for the revolution. Like many, I was expecting to die any time in shelling or air strikes or at the hands of Hezbollah fighters. I was content with that destiny because ours was a battle against dictatorship and injustice. But when my life was threatened by an armed group that claimed to be fighting for our freedom, I realized that things were not black-and-white anymore. I started to ask if risking death was really worth it.

The final straw came about two weeks after I got married. We woke up one morning to a massive explosion. There was screaming, dust, and my wife's desperate cries. I found myself immobilized and realized that the cabinets and window had collapsed on top of us and were pinning us down. In our darkest hour, luck was on our side: we were sleeping with two thick blankets, and they protected us from the glass and rubble that littered the room. Not everyone had our luck. I don't remember how many people died that day, but everyone in the family on the top floor of our building was killed.

We moved what was left of our belongings to my uncle's house and started searching for a way to evacuate to Lebanon. It took us a month to find a vehicle. That was the first time we traveled "abroad." In Lebanon, we moved again from one place to another. Moving became easier and easier each time.

Okba

SALAMIYAH, SYRIA

When everything began in 2011, my heart was with the opposition. My fiancée, Siba, was the same, but her family was afraid and wanted nothing to do with politics. Her father said that we shouldn't get married until the political situation was resolved. He was afraid. Maybe I would do my mandatory military service and get killed?

My brother was doing his military service, posted in an office job. After a year, they wanted to send him to fight. He came home for his vacation for three days and then went back to the base by motorbike. Normally when he arrived at the base, he'd call to say that everything was okay. But this time he didn't call. Two days went by. My father tried to call him, and nobody answered. Then my father called my brother's supervising officer. He said that my brother had never returned. I asked around, but nobody knew anything.

After one week, someone called us and said, "We are the opposition. We have your son and we're going to kill him because he chose not to defect from the army." They hung up and then wouldn't answer when we tried to call back. We went to the police and they said, "They're terrorists, there's nothing we can do." My father cried when he talked to them. My mother wept so much that we had to take her to the hospital.

Ten days later, my brother called. He explained that he had just pretended that he was kidnapped so he could defect from the army. What he did was very clever. We'd been so upset that now everyone would believe us that he was actually kidnapped. He hid in another town, where there were a lot of people who'd left the army. He joined the Free Syrian Army* but didn't really want to participate in the war. He said, "I don't want to fight for the army, but that doesn't mean I want to fight for the other side. I just want to quit." Eventually, he decided to smuggle himself to Turkey.

☺

SOMETIME AFTER that, the Islamic State† came along. Everyone was astonished by how IS got all this money and weapons when the Free Syrian Army didn't receive anything. IS took Palmyra and villages near my city. Many people who were protesting the government started to hope that the government wouldn't leave after all. They were afraid that IS would come and massacre us because, for them, we're infidels. It didn't matter if you're Muslim or not. They killed everyone who didn't agree with them.

But something strange happened. The government didn't try to retake those villages. It didn't fight IS like it fought the Free Syrian Army. Assad just let IS come near our city so he could say to the media, "Look, the opposition are terrorists." Every few months, IS would launch two or three rockets on the city, but that was it.

---

* In July 2011, after four months of overwhelmingly unarmed demonstrations, defectors from Syria's conscript-based military, along with civilian opposition-ists, announced the formation of the Free Syrian Army to take up arms to fight the Assad regime. Though it never cohered as a fighting force under a single command and control, the Free Syrian Army succeeded in pushing Assad's forces from large swaths of the country.

† In January 2011, al-Qaeda members, some of whom had earlier entered Syria from Iraq, formed al-Nusra Front with the goal of replacing the Assad regime with an Islamic caliphate. In 2013, a rift between al-Nusra and al-Qaeda led to the formation of a new group: the Islamic State in Iraq and Syria (ISIS). Bolstered by foreign fighters, ISIS conquered thousands of miles of territory across northern Syria and imposed its own brutal rule on civilians. In 2014, after crossing the border and seizing parts of western Iraq, ISIS declared itself to be the Islamic State (IS).

◎

I GOT a job with an organization that worked in areas under rebel control. I coordinated projects on things like transparency, transitional justice, and organization development. For example, some villages or cities in opposition-controlled areas wanted to have elections for local councils, so we had workshops to train people to be election observers.

The organization's headquarters were in Gaziantep, Turkey. I'd travel there to attend workshops and then come back and apply what I'd learned. It wasn't easy to travel to Turkey. I couldn't go north across the border because IS was there. Instead, I'd go by bus to Lebanon, fly to Istanbul, and then fly from Istanbul to Gaziantep.

For the Syrian government, Turkey was the enemy and our work was illegal. If you work for an organization with the word "democracy" in its name, you're a terrorist. The first time I traveled and returned to Syria, the border officer saw the Turkish stamp in my passport and said, "What were you doing in Turkey?" I was really afraid. Thank God, the driver of the bus I was on paid a bribe, and the officers let me go through. Another time, I faked a paper that said that I was registered at a university in Istanbul. Another time when I went to Turkey, my colleague was supposed to follow me there, and the Syrian military arrested him at the border. I was very afraid. Maybe the army knew about our work? I decided to stay in Turkey until we learned what had happened to him. Two months went by. We heard nothing.

◎

FROM TIME to time, the Military Intelligence Service would come to my parents' house and ask if they knew anything about my brother. Once, Military Intelligence asked about me. My father was afraid to say that I was in Turkey. He said, "Okba is in the Netherlands." It just came out. They said, "What is he doing there?" My father said that I was getting a master's degree. That was always my dream, actually, and it's just what came to his mind.

And that's how I decided not to go back to Syria. I discussed it with Siba. Should I tell her family the truth about what happened? They didn't want anything to do with politics. If they knew about my situation, they would say that our relationship was finished. So, we decided to lie too. She told her family, "Okba traveled to the Netherlands." Her father is a kind and simple man, but he was very angry. "How the hell did he go to the Netherlands all of a sudden without even talking to us?" I went to a park in Gaziantep and called him on Skype so he could see the trees around me. I talked to him about how beautiful it was in the Netherlands and how difficult the language was.

My father thought, "Okay, let's make the story official." He started to tell everyone, "Okba went to the Netherlands." Many friends sent me messages like, "You asshole, how did you go to the Netherlands without telling us?"

Maha

HOMS, SYRIA

My husband would lock the door and sleep next to it so our son Mazer couldn't go to protests. But Mazer would manage to get out, and our daughter Hala would throw him his clothes and shoes from the balcony.

At that time, my oldest son, Mohammed, was doing his compulsory military service. He didn't want to kill people, but if he didn't stay in the army, the regime would kill him. Eventually, he decided to defect. He asked me to send him money so he would have an excuse to leave the military base and go collect it. He took the money and escaped to Homs, where our family is from.

His officers called us the next morning and asked where Mohammed was. If I'd been awake, I would have said, "He's with you." But Hala answered the phone. I'd forgotten to tell her not to do that. She was so afraid that she said, "I don't know," and hung up.

We had to move. Immediately. They could detain any of us. We moved to Daraya in the Damascus suburbs. Hardly a week passed before tanks entered and started firing at protestors. We moved to Damascus. Later they started searching for our kids at school. We moved houses again. My daughter Insaf had to quit attending university because it wasn't safe.

Homs was under siege. My brother was killed, hit by an airstrike just five months after he was married. They detained my cousin and returned her body to her mother. My aunt said that it wasn't her daughter, but she had to pretend that it was. To this day, she doesn't know where her daughter is.

After a month or two, Mohammed was wounded in his stomach by an exploding bullet. They did surgery in someone's house. A general doctor did it because there were no specialists around. If Mohammed had gone to the hospital, they would have killed him.

God gave me courage and strength, and I went to Homs to get Mohammed out. The doctor gave him a tranquilizer and we left. My friend came with me, and we brought her son's passport for Mohammed to use at checkpoints. I was terrified. It was the longest trip of my life. It was only two hours, but it felt like two days. There was a checkpoint practically every five hundred meters, but the rain was so heavy that soldiers hardly stopped the cars.

We reached Damascus. The first day passed and then the second, and Mohammed's wound became infected. A doctor would secretly come and check on him, bringing an ultrasound machine in a garbage bag so no one suspected anything. Once the doctor couldn't make it, so he sent a newly graduated medical student. The student saw Mohammed's wound and started shaking. We had to tell him, "Do this here," or, "Try that." I'll never forget the look on his face. To be honest, we were afraid he would report us.

We were staying in an apartment owned by people who supported the revolution. They gave us a phone and told us that if it ever rang just once, that meant the police were coming and we needed to leave. The apartment didn't get any sunlight, so we lived in the dark, in fear. We hardly went outside. If Mohammed heard as much as a spoon drop while he slept, he'd shoot awake, thinking that the regime was there. People would steal bandages from the hospital for us. If we bought any from a store, they'd be suspicious.

Mohammed's situation got worse. The wound was so infected that it leaked pus. The smell was unbearable. He was begging for someone to change his bandages. I couldn't bring myself to do it. His father couldn't either. Insaf was about nineteen then, and she said, "I'll do it." His sister became his nurse. One day when Insaf was changing the bandages, she screamed. I swear to God that I'll never forget that scream.

She said, "Mom, part of his intestines came out." What did she mean, "part of his intestines"? When she was cleaning the wound, the pus had massed together and looked like intestines.

Mohammed would scream in pain, banging the walls. We finally took him to the hospital for another surgery, using a fake name. They did the surgery in the basement because if they did it on the main floor, the regime would find out. The doctors finished and said, "Now, get him out of here."

But Mohammed's wounds began to open again. He needed another surgery. That's when we decided that he needed to leave the country. He was going to die. He had no chance if he stayed. We talked with the rebels, and they said that they would get him out. God sent good people. They spoke in code on the phone, telling us, "Get the groom ready."

They came for him at three o'clock in the morning. Mohammed spent one night at the border and then had to walk two or three hours into Jordan. He later told me that, to motivate himself to walk, he imagined that Bashar al-Assad himself was in front of him and he was trying to grab him. When they told Mohammed that he was safe in Jordan, he passed out.

Once I knew Mohammed was safe, I said, "That's it, they're going to kidnap the girls and the rest of us. We have to leave too." We called the guys who got Mohammed out. They told us to get ready.

Hani

DEIR EZ-ZOR, SYRIA

I decided to defect from the army. My brother told me, "Come home to Deir ez-Zor, but don't say anything to anybody. It's too dangerous. Don't even tell Mom and Dad."

My brother knew a lot of people in rebel groups. He took me to an apartment with people I'd never seen in my life. I thought, "I'm here because I can't be in the army and I can't go anywhere else." You do what you have to do.

There was a military commander named Abu Jaber, and we became really close. We used to sleep in the same apartment on the front line. He gave me that feeling: "You're safe with me. Nothing is going to happen to you." There was a window air-conditioning unit. At night the government would bomb, and the cardboard stuck in the window for the AC would fall on us. Abu Jaber would get up, put the cardboard back, and fall right back to sleep. We lived like it was the two of us against the world. We felt like we were in this together. Together, we could win. I broke my army tag in half and gave one piece to him and kept the other.

But it was a terrible life. The army was surrounding the area more and more each day. The city felt so tight. The people living in the area were sympathetic, but we felt that nobody wanted us around them. We moved from house to house, not knowing where to go. We got stuck in one room for a few months. I didn't see the sun the whole time.

○

ONCE, ONE of the guys in the group went home for a few days and came back with new thoughts. He said, "I want to make my own group."

The guys started arguing, and it became an actual physical fight. This guy had his people, and the other guys had everybody else. They started shooting. Grenades were rolling on the ground. That was the moment that I thought, "That's it. I'm done." I didn't want something to happen to me because these guys don't like each other. That is not a reason to die. I said, "I want out of here. That's it."

I decided to go to Turkey. I didn't know anybody. I had no plan. I told everyone, "I only want to see Abu Jaber before I leave." Abu Jaber was avoiding me. Then I ran into him while I were preparing to leave the city, and he said, "Well, you're going to Turkey and leaving me behind." He joked, "Go enjoy life. Go drink and find a girlfriend."

I said, "No, man, come on. I'm done with this. I'm so tired, I can't take it anymore."

And I left. The group I traveled with had a really complicated trip. It's five hundred kilometers—three days in the desert. We saw the flag of the Syrian Army at some point, which was terrifying. One smuggler handed us to somebody, who handed us to somebody else and then somebody else. You don't know anything about these people. They might actually turn you in to the army. You have no choice but to trust them.

Sixteen days after we made it to Turkey, Abu Jaber was killed in battle. Not even like three or four months later. Sixteen days. He stayed and died. I left and lived. And this is the guilt I live with every day.

Alaa

AL-QUSAYR, SYRIA

The country became a war zone. I was seventeen. At that time, the hardest thing was deciding to stay or leave. You can't imagine how hard that decision was. Some people left. We stayed. The bombardment got more intense, with planes, missiles, and shelling. Finally, we decided to secure safe passage for the women in the family who wanted to get out. My mom and sisters left. Then it was just me, my brother, my father, my uncle and his son, and my other uncle and his son.

The seven of us lived together. We ate every meal together. We developed an unnaturally strong attachment to each other. We said that we'd stay until the battles waned because we hoped the opposition would win. But the regime used the same Russian methods that they used on other towns: scorched-earth assault, siege, invade. The first invasion attempt came from the south, so we moved to a neighborhood in the north of town. Our ears got tired from hearing missiles all day. Staying in basement shelters was exhausting.

We feared that the town was going to fall and there would be massacres. We wanted to get out, but the siege was insane and no cars were entering or leaving. The main roads were controlled by the regime, so we went by foot on a dirt road. Imagine: You're carrying a bag on your back, leaving in the dark of night. People are trying to get you to the other side. Your brain tells you that you are leaving this home and not coming back. The worst thing is if the road is closed and you have to return home again.

The first time didn't work. We tried a second time and then a third time. We were seven people and everyone had the proper papers. We thought, "God willing, we'll get through." That was June 1st, which was supposed to be the day of my high school completion exam. I'd studied really hard but didn't get to take it.

We left in a minibus and reached the second checkpoint to the east of town. There, they took our papers and looked up our names. At that point, there was no going back. And that's when we were arrested.

THEY BLINDFOLDED all seven of us and took us to Military Security. My cousins and I were put with people our age. My dad and uncles were taken to a different cell. The cells were one meter by sixty centimeters. It was very hot and we were basically naked. They gave you just a few seconds to run to the bathroom and would beat you on the way.

On the sixth day, my brother's name came up for interrogation. Then my cousin, then me, then my other cousin. They interrogated us again the next day, the day after, and the day after that. The interrogator asked me what I did. You had to say that you did something. You couldn't just say that you attended a demonstration because that wouldn't be enough for them. But you also had to steer clear of big crimes like attacking a checkpoint or something. You needed to find something in between that would convince them. You had to weigh every word carefully. For example, once I said, "And then we were arrested at the checkpoint." The interrogator said, "You weren't *arrested*, you were stopped." The interrogator asked me for names of people against the regime. That was a dilemma. I gave him the names of people who were dead or who were out of the country or who would never go to regime-controlled areas where they might get caught.

They moved the four of us to a cell with my dad and uncles. After a few days, they called my name. Only my name. I looked at the six others and said goodbye.

I THOUGHT I was being released. Instead, I was moved to another security branch. Every time I was interrogated, I repeated the same story. I was accused of vandalism and destroying buildings, which was better than protesting or murder.

They took me to different courts to be tried. During my trial, a lawyer told me that one of my detained uncles had been killed. I was in shock. When you hear this kind of news, your brain just rejects it.

I was moved to the central prison. Others there had been transferred from Military Security too. They would say, "I saw this person dead, that person alive, this person transferred." That's when I heard a rumor that all of my family members in prison had been killed, except for my brother and one cousin. Again, my brain rejected it. "Impossible. It can't be."

After forty-one days in prison, I was released. By that time, my town didn't exist anymore. It was destroyed, leveled. I went to another town where I had family, and my mom met me there. I redid my last year of high school and got my diploma. I started dental school, and we moved again so I could get to campus without crossing checkpoints. Every day there was fear of what tomorrow would bring. At any time, the regime could do a raid and take you for interrogation.

I didn't tell my mom or anyone else in my family what I'd heard about our family members who were detained. They'd ask me and I'd act like I didn't know. I didn't want to deliver that news. Besides, I didn't have proof. Maybe they could end up being alive or released? Your brain convinces you to wait. "Just wait, wait. Tomorrow will be better than today." I'd heard about my dad, but still hoped to hear good news about my brother. Then I could tell my mom the good news and bad news at the same time. I figured the same thing about my cousin: maybe his mom would get good news about her son, and at that time I could tell her that her husband had been martyred.

I tried to come to terms with it. I tried not to think about it all the time. But you couldn't escape it. It was a never-ending cycle of dark thoughts. And then, at some point, my uncle living in Lebanon received official papers with the names of my dad, my uncles, and my cousin, saying that they were all dead. I had another uncle in Syria. One day they knocked on his door and said, "Come with us." And then he was detained, as well.

My family urged me to leave. They feared that it was just a matter of time before they knocked on our door, as well. The charges were ready. I didn't have a passport, and even going to apply for one could get me detained. I paid a lawyer who took responsibility for taking me from office to office to fill out the passport paperwork. At every turn: corruption, corruption, corruption. Bribes ran everything.

I got the passport and booked a trip. On October 31st, I left for Lebanon. From there, I took a ship to Mersin, Turkey and then a bus to Izmir. By November 2nd, I was in Greece. It took three hours to cross the sea. I was leaving death. You're running from hell. Whatever is ahead of you is better than what you left behind. Now people ask me, "Were you afraid on the boat?" That makes me laugh every time. After everything I'd seen in Syria, how could I be afraid of a boat?

II

LEAVING, AGAIN

SARA M., MAHA, OKBA, KOVAN,
MOHAMMED W., MANAF, MEDEA

In the early years of the war, many who crossed by land from Syria into Jordan, Lebanon, Turkey, or Iraq hardly thought of themselves as refugees. Rather, they had left home temporarily to wait for the lull in violence that they expected would come any day. Then days became weeks, weeks became months, and months became years.

This dilemma of extended displacement affects refugees around the world, including some who are born, raised, and then have children and grandchildren of their own in refugee camps. Recognizing that "no one wants to be a refugee their whole life," UNHCR advocates for what it calls three "durable solutions": refugees voluntarily return to their home country if the situation is safe; they integrate into their country of refuge, culminating in citizenship; or they resettle in a third country that agrees to admit them and ultimately grant permanent residence.

In the Syrian case, the first solution remains inappropriate. The United Nations (UN) and human rights groups judge Syria to be unsafe, and the very small number of refugees who have opted to return testifies that displaced Syrians agree. Prospects for the second solution, local integration, are severely limited in countries in the Middle East.

With the exception of Turkey's controversial awarding of nationality to about 200,000 select Syrians, nearly all of the 5.5 million Syrian refugees in the Middle East have "guest" status, entailing temporary protection but no guarantee of permanent residency. The legal rights necessary for genuine long-term integration thus do not exist. The third solution is similarly unattainable. Syrians have joined the millions of other refugees worldwide who apply to UNHCR each year in pursuit of safe, legal resettlement to a wealthy country. Yet fewer than 1 percent of all refugees are ever chosen for this coveted opportunity.[1]

For the vast majority of people who flee Syria, therefore, none of the UN's durable solutions are within reach. Instead, they devise solutions of their own. Some move from one country in the Middle East to another, searching for better conditions. Some obtain scholarships to study elsewhere, hoping that a student visa might open a pathway to a longer-term future. Some with international familial relations get visas for legal travel. If Syrians can step foot in a country that offers opportunities for asylum, they have a good chance of demonstrating a well-founded fear of harm in their home country and gaining rights to permanent residency or at least temporary protection status. The European Union (EU) is a geographically proximate place that accepts asylum applications. Obtaining a visa to travel there on a Syrian passport, however, is akin to winning the lottery.

It is in this context that some asylum-seekers rally all the savings and savvy that they can and risk their lives to reach the countries that go to lengths to prevent their entry. At first, those who dared to cross to Europe by sea typically made the long, arduous journey from Egypt or Libya to Italy. Around 2015, accumulating crises across the Middle East and Africa accelerated rates of travel across the shorter and safer route from Turkey to Greece. Smugglers proliferated, charging thousands of dollars per person to pile migrants into flimsy boats and inflatable dinghies. While thousands drowned, more than a million refugees made it ashore and launched treacherous treks north and westward. Some countries raised razor wire at their borders. German Chancellor Angela Merkel suspended the protocol that would return Syrian refugees to their first EU country of entry, effectively extending safe haven to those who could make it to Germany. Migration sowed panic across the EU until early 2016, when Turkey agreed to block illicit migration from its territory in exchange for billions of euros and other benefits. Thereafter, an annual average of at least 120,000 refugees and migrants would continue to attempt to cross the Mediterranean, mostly on the more lethal passage from North Africa. From 2014 until 2023, more than 54,000 migrants went missing or were confirmed dead at sea.

The narratives to follow build on earlier stories about leaving Syria and explore what it is like, having arrived in a first country of refuge, to leave again. Sara M. says a second goodbye to her activist twin Abu Tarek, dons a disguise, and sneaks across the border to Turkey. Maha, relieved as her son Mohammed recovers from his injuries, moves with the rest of her family to Jordan and then braves the boat trip across the sea. Having convinced everyone back home that he is in the Netherlands, Okba searches for ways to remain in Turkey before plotting to reach the Netherlands, for real. Kovan also sets his sights on northern Europe, but his voyage hits a roadblock when he is arrested in Greece. No longer able to tolerate life in a squalid informal settlement in Lebanon, Mohammed W. becomes ready to pay any price for a ticket out. Manaf's planned Mediterranean escape is thwarted, but his disappointment unexpectedly leads to something better. While most of these individuals go to lengths to move onward from their initial stop after Syria, Medea's sorrow in departing Egypt reminds us that this is not always the case. When one comes into one's own in a new place, leaving again can be as hard as leaving the first time.

Experiences of transiting from a temporary refuge to a potentially permanent settlement serve as part of the connective tissue between past and future homes. They are not simply pauses and delays in the search for home, but part of what makes home a struggle and achievement. People might search for home numerous times in multiple places. Luck, money, connections, despair, courage, and know-how all combine to determine how far they go. Long travels under perilous conditions can entrench a deep sense of insecurity that is hard to shake even after the voyage ends. Indeed, one might feel that the voyage never ends, even when one is no longer physically on the move. For these and other reasons, migrants' and refugees' journeys can leave enduring imprints on their relationship to home. They might intensify one's longing for a stable anchor or leave one doubting that such an anchor exists. In coping with rootlessness en route to the next stage of life, people gain new perspectives on what it means to have roots and whether, ultimately, they need them.

Sara M.

GAZIANTEP, TURKEY

After I got turned away at the border, I went back to Damascus and explained what happened. I told Abu Tarek, "If I get arrested, you're next, boss. You'll be the first one I name when I have to confess."

I stayed for just one week. The guys arranged for me to go to Turkey through Idlib, which was no longer under regime control. They paid a smuggler. I used the ID of another young woman. Her eyes were brown and mine are light, so the guys got me colored contact lenses. I dressed up like a Druze sheikha, wearing a black abaya and a hijab and a white covering over my nose and the mouth.* Security forces wouldn't dare tell a sheikha to uncover her face, or they might have problems with the Druze. Whenever anyone asked my name, I said it was Um Muhammed.

We passed through so many checkpoints. At each, the driver gave the soldiers money and cigarettes so they wouldn't check our IDs. We left regime-controlled areas and crossed into areas controlled by al-

---

* Druze, an ethnoreligious group with a faith combining diverse religious and philosophical sources, constitute approximately 3 percent of the Syrian population. Since 2011, the Assad regime has sought to preserve the community's loyalty or at least its neutrality in the war. It has done so by wielding different forms of violent intimidation, as well as by granting the community subsidies and a measure of autonomy in managing its own affairs.

Nusra Front. I changed to a black covering over my face. I spent one day on the road to Idlib, a day and a night in a village, another night in another village, and then I left for Turkey. I'd been told that I'd take a bus and then walk for a while and then take a second bus.

It started to rain. The bus got stuck in mud and couldn't move. It was nine o'clock at night when we got out and started walking. For the next nine hours we walked up the mountains and down into valleys. My boots were covered with mud. I couldn't hear a thing except the sound of my heartbeat and breath. There was a family with me: a father, mother, and three-year-old girl who cried the whole time. There was no one else in the area. Only God and the smuggler.

We walked on a very narrow path that was barely as wide as my own feet. We held on to thorny bushes. Underfoot was mud and darkness. By the end, I could no longer lift my boots. I took them off and started walking in bare feet. We kept walking until we arrived at a road that separates Syria and Turkey. We saw the border and ran across.

Maha

AMMAN, JORDAN

In Jordan, they placed Mohammed in a camp for military defectors. He had access to medicine and healed in three months, thank God.

Our life in Jordan was hard. Hala went to school, Insaf enrolled again in the university. But my husband couldn't find work. We ran out of money and Insaf had to drop out. We left for Turkey, but life was hard there too. We couldn't find work. Insaf and Hala taught English, but I wanted them to study, not just survive.

We decided to try to migrate to Europe. We made a deal with a smuggler. There were sixty-five people on the boat. I sat cross-legged. My youngest, Mahmoud, was on my lap, and two people were on top of him. Mahmoud cried the whole trip. We were at sea for about an hour when the motor died. We heard the wood of the boat cracking, and water filled up to my chest. The most difficult thing is to feel that your family is going to die right in front of you. You pray, "Please let us all live or let us all die. Or let me die before they do."

The Red Cross came, but they couldn't tow our boat because it was breaking apart. They called the coast guard, and after a while a barge came. We were drenched in water. After sitting cross-legged for so long, I couldn't get up. Insaf and Hala couldn't get out either. They started pulling us out by our arms. Two of my tendons tore. When I saw a doctor years later, he said it looked like I'd been in a car accident.

In Lesbos, volunteers were waiting for us. We made it to Athens on the third day, but they told us that the border with Macedonia was closed. We went there anyway, but it was a disaster. Insaf got sick, Hala got sick, Mahmoud had a fever and was hallucinating and vomiting. We were tired and dirty.

A journalist told us that we should take a bus to Thessaloniki. The bus driver spoke to the girls in English and said, "Thessaloniki is expensive. Instead, come to my village. It's cheaper." We agreed and got in the bus but were afraid. We thought he might be kidnapping us. After an hour or so, we arrived in his village. The people found us a vacant house and brought us everything: clothes, food, bedding. The bus driver brought us hot soup, and it was the best thing I'd ever tasted.

They told us that we could use Skype to sign up for a program. We went to a volunteer's hotel room to use the Internet and tried Skype nineteen times before it connected. When a lady answered, it felt like my heart stopped. She took down our information and that was it.

We waited. We were lost. The kids carried a burden that they were too young to carry. My husband and I should have carried it, but we shared it with them. Insaf was always lying on a mattress on the floor. She would see the mountains near the village and say, "If no country lets us in, we can go live in a cave." I told her, "No. I promise we'll get somewhere better."

About two months later, we got a call from a strange number. Insaf went to a neighbor and used her phone to call back. They answered, "French Embassy." We were clapping, crying, laughing, screaming. We thought, "This is it! We're going to France. France!" But they were just giving us an appointment. We still needed an interview.

They interviewed each of us separately. The questions were weird, like, "Do you pray? Do you fast? Do you go the mosque? What are your thoughts on jihad?" Hala responded, "What's jihad?" I can't describe the fear we felt. If any of us made a mistake in any detail, there would be no trip. Sometimes Insaf's leg shakes when she talks. The interviewer said, "Why are you shaking your leg? It means you're lying." She was so afraid that she'd make a mistake and be the reason that we didn't travel.

The official told us, "Now you have to wait for approval." We'd thought that we were going to France that day. We were at the breaking

point, but we waited. After fifteen days, they called and said, "Congrat-
ulations, France approved your application."

We waited another full month after that. The whole time we said,
"Maybe we'll go tomorrow. Or maybe it won't happen at all." We still
couldn't believe that there was a future for us. We thought, for sure,
some problem would inevitably come up.

Okba

GAZIANTEP, TURKEY

I stayed in Gaziantep for three months. The whole time, I kept telling everyone in Syria that I was in the Netherlands. I was terrified that someone would find out that wasn't true. I feared for my family's safety. I deactivated my Facebook account because sometimes when you write a message, it indicates your location. Eventually, I blocked all my contacts.

My brother was in Istanbul, and his situation was no better. As a Syrian without papers, he was working underground in a textile factory. He earned about two hundred and fifty dollars a month and lived with four other guys in a very small room. I visited him at the factory, but he wasn't able to leave the machines and go outside, so I sat with him in the basement. It was very dark and very loud. I couldn't imagine how he stayed there twelve or thirteen hours a day, listening to all that noise. Still, I asked if I could get a job there too. They said that they didn't need more workers.

After three months, my residency permit was about to expire. My Syrian passport had only six months left. Soon, I'd be illegal in Turkey. I started to hear about refugees going to Europe. But you needed three to four thousand dollars. I talked to my father, and he decided to sell the small shop we owned. When my aunt heard that, she gave us the money instead.

I went to Izmir and contacted a smuggler. Every day he said, "Yeah, tomorrow." After nineteen days, he took a group of sixteen of us to the location. The smuggler told us to go into the water to reach the boat. When the boat came, it was not a big luxury yacht like he said. It was a rubber dinghy. And there were no life jackets, which was like a horror movie for me because I don't know how to swim.

I decided not to go. The others did the same. The smuggler was very angry. He yelled, "If you don't go, I'll tell the police that there are illegal Syrians here, and they'll arrest you." We were very scared and just ran into the woods. That was one of the worst nights of my life. Everything was wet. When I went into the water, I didn't even think about the fact that my mobile phone was in my pocket. It also got wet and stopped working.

We stayed among the trees until morning when someone came and said that the smuggler had brought life jackets. We went back. I thought, "It doesn't matter anymore. I've already lost everything. I might as well go."

◎

WE WERE on the water for five to six hours and had no idea where we were going. I was so afraid that I prayed to all gods in all religions. I thought only about my mother. What would she do if I never called her again?

We made it to an island called Chios, and then I got to Athens. From there, you have two options. The first is to go north through Macedonia. If you're caught in Macedonia, they take you to jail, make you pay a thousand-dollar fine, and send you back to Greece. If you're successful in Macedonia, then you have Serbia. There are army checkpoints on the border, and if you get caught, they beat you and take all of your money, put you in prison, and send you back to Macedonia. To avoid the police, some refugees try to cross through the forests. But the forests are filled with armed gangs who will rob or kill you. And anyway, after Serbia you have Hungary, where border security is very tough.

That's the first option. The second option is very easy. You pay a smuggler, and he gets you a fake European ID and a cheap flight. You just go to the airport and try to fly to another European country. If you don't succeed, you try again or ask for your money back.

So that's what I did. The first time, I got an Italian ID and a flight to Rome. At the first checkpoint in the airport, I gave them the ID. They asked me in English, "Are you Italian?"

"Yes!"

"You speak Italian?"

"Yes!"

The man called a colleague who started to speak to me in Italian. I looked at him like a fool. They shouted and threw me out of the airport.

☙

I STAYED in Athens for three months. Eight times I bought ID cards for different European countries. Every time, I got caught in the airport. I don't know how they figured out that I'm not European!

In early December, the smuggler got me a flight from Rhodes to Sweden. He said that Rhodes is a smaller airport, which means less control and better chances. I took a big ship like fourteen hours from Athens to Rhodes. At the airport, I went to the gate and showed the lady my boarding pass. I smiled and waited in line. My heart was beating so fast. I thought, "It's been almost six months since I left Syria, and soon I'll be in Stockholm." I thought about it more. "Maybe I'll just stay there. I'll tell everyone 'I was in the Netherlands, but there were better opportunities in Sweden, so I changed my country.'"

I was very happy as I lost myself in those thoughts. And then suddenly someone touched my shoulder from behind. "Hey, I'm talking to you. ID card?"

I gave him my ID card.

"Ah, Sweden. What's your name?"

Why did this smuggler choose a Swedish name that was so hard to remember? The name on the ID was very complicated. I wanted to ask the guy, "Hey, can I look at the ID again so I can see my name?"

The guy started shouting and threw me out.

At the main door of the airport, I started to cry. That was the first time I really cried. I was thinking "Why did I come here?" I was all alone. For months, I'd been calling Siba's parents and telling them about the Netherlands. What was I doing? I went back to Athens and told the smuggler, "Give me my money back. I'm heading north."

⊙

I WENT to Thessaloniki. I learned that you need to take a train to Polykastro. From there, you walk like ten hours to Evzonoi. Then you cross into Macedonia. I set off with a group. I didn't know what was waiting for me after the next hour or the next kilometer. But I felt more optimistic because I was no longer just waiting. I was doing something.

We reached the borders and got caught by the police. Fortunately, it was the Greek police, and they sent us back to Thessaloniki. I tried again and managed to reach Evzonoi. There I joined another group of people. After three days, a smuggler got us across Macedonia and then all the way to the border with Serbia. The smuggler said, "Pay four hundred dollars. We'll walk about three hours and then drive to Belgrade." It was December and very cold. We were twenty people and started walking. Four hours, eight hours, ten hours. And then the smuggler said, "Okay, we have to stay overnight in the woods." It took us maybe six hours to make a fire because the wood was all wet. Thank God, there were some smokers with us who had lighters.

The next day, we woke up and couldn't find the smuggler anywhere. It started to snow, and we didn't have any food or water. We started to eat snow. I don't recommend it. We were completely wet and started walking. Near nightfall we reached a small village not far from Kosovo. We found a mosque and it was unlocked, so we entered and slept. In the early morning, people from the village came for the dawn prayer. They saw us and tried to speak to us in Serbian. They did the prayer and left. I thought they were going to call the police. But about fifteen minutes later, they came back with food and water and clean shoes and socks. It was heaven. They used hand and face gestures to communicate that we should hurry because the police might come. Then they drove us to another village and bought us tickets for a bus to Belgrade. If only I'd known that it was so easy! We didn't even need a smuggler. We could simply take a bus.

I hope you won't ever have to make it as a refugee but, just in case, I'll give you some tips. Buy at least three extra phone batteries and charge them in Athens before you head out. When you get to Macedonia, buy a SIM card so you have Internet. But when you're in a group, not everyone has to switch on their mobiles. One is enough. Use Google Maps. Without Google Maps, I probably wouldn't be talking to you right now.

☉

WE CONTINUED: Belgrade, Hungary, Austria. When I reached Vienna, I had like twenty-five euros left. I thought: "I can't continue to the Netherlands. Maybe I'll stay here. My family can tell everyone, 'Okba was in the Netherlands, but his university was very hard, so he found another opportunity in Austria.' "

One of the guys in our group had a cousin in Germany, so he bought a train ticket to go there. The others said that they'd also go to Germany. I thought, "I can't stay here by myself." I decided to go to Germany too. I had no money, so I entered the train without a ticket. It was around New Year's Day, and a lot of people were traveling. I figured security would be light.

On the train, everything was fine. I thought, "Maybe I'll just take trains all the way to the Netherlands." Then we crossed the border and the German police entered. They spotted me right away and said, "ID card, please."

Kovan

KOMOTINI, GREECE

I was just trying to get to Sweden, where some family members lived. I paid a bribe at the border and went to Turkey. After ten days, I crossed the river to Greece. That's where the police caught me.

I stayed in prison in Greece for three months and ten days. Sometimes there wasn't enough food, and sometimes there was no food at all. We stayed in a stable that had been used for cows or horses, and there were no lights at night. We had outdoor time once a week. I don't think I saw myself in a mirror the whole time. But prison was also a beautiful school. There were people from all over the world. You can't ignore others in prison; you're forced to be friends and that introduces you to wonderful things from other cultures. We had no common language but understood one another with gestures. There was a Pakistani guy who always sang in Urdu, and I'd whistle along with the same tune.

Some of the police who guarded the prison were racist, and some were good. I learned some Greek and became friendly with a few of the officers who guarded the prison. There was a market once a week. If you had money, you could write out what you wanted, and the police would bring it. Once I was smoking with a cop and I said, "Honestly, I'm craving eggs, I haven't eaten eggs in so long." The next day he brought eggs and said, "My mom cooked these for you." It was such a gift.

I got out of prison and stayed in Greece another three months. I was afraid the entire time, both inside prison and out. Not having a passport is really, really scary. You try to act normal but you're always insecure. You walk down the street and feel like you're committing a crime. You cross the street and feel like you're committing a crime. Your mere presence is illegal.

I found a smuggler who got me a forged passport. I went to the airport, but it didn't work. Then he realized I spoke some Greek. He said, "I'm going to get you a real Greek passport, and we'll just change the picture." He gave me the passport of an Iraqi guy who had lived in Greece. At the airport, the police stopped me. I started speaking in Greek and they let me through. It was my first time on an airplane. When the plane first took off, it felt like my heart stopped. I couldn't tell if I was afraid of flying or afraid of the police.

Mohammed W.

ARSAL, LEBANON

If you ascend to the peak of the mountain in Arsal, you see clear skies and white clouds. Arsal will seem like a white spot below. But it's not a white spot. It's a collection of tents.

The Syrian refugee camps in Lebanon are on rented land.* We owned the tent and paid rent to a Lebanese landlord for the space we occupied. The Lebanese government prevented us from building anything to protect ourselves. They'd say, "We're against permanent settlement." But a tent is like a bag, nothing more. And this area can get a lot of snow. Children died of the cold.

My mom and sisters left for Lebanon before I did. When I first got to Arsal, I was surprised to find them without even a mattress to sleep on. They folded their clothes and used them under their heads as pillows.

---

* Hundreds of thousands of Syrian refugees in Lebanon live in informal camps or settlements, often squalid and unserviced clusters of tents or shacks on privately rented land. Lebanon has not built official state- or UN-sponsored refugee camps for Syrian refugees on the grounds that formal camps might become permanent, as was the case for the camps that were constructed for Palestinians who were forced to flee their homeland in 1948 and that exist until today. Lebanon's policies toward Syrian refugees are further complicated by its own difficult history with Syria. Hafez al-Assad sent troops to Lebanon in 1976 during the early years of the Lebanese civil war, and Syria continued to occupy the country until mass protests in Lebanon compelled its withdrawal in 2005.

But the biggest surprise was when I entered the camp itself. There are two hundred and fifteen tents and about six hundred and fifty people in the camp. Every tent has a toilet. There isn't an underground sewage network, so people dig holes under the toilets like in the old days. The sewage holes are near the water wells, and sewage contaminates the drinking water. Sewage also flows between the tents. When I lived in the camp, I could always smell the camp on my body.

These were bitter days. As a man who defected from the Syrian Army, I didn't dare leave Arsal. During my eight years in Lebanon, I never visited Beirut. Not once. Any sound at night or car that passed would terrify me. I thought, "Hezbollah is coming for me." It was terror. Fear lived alongside us. Fear of uncertainty. Fear of what comes next. Even if I had nothing to fear, my subconscious would start imagining things because I was so used to feeling afraid.

In your brain, there's something called the amygdala and the hippocampus. During a traumatic event, your brain gets overwhelmed and those parts don't work normally. If everything in my brain was normal, I'd be in control. But my brain stored old traumas like photographs. When I see a trigger, I start recalling things like a camera. I won't be thinking of Syria or Lebanon or anything and then, with one word or situation or movement, the emotions start. Emotions of anxiety, of worry, of fear.

Fear is suffocating. Suffocating. You can't control anything. Fear, because I lost everything. Fear that, if I became attached to someone, I might lose them. I was in love for six years and she died because of the war. The war taught us that we shouldn't love anyone. The war taught us: Save yourself. Save yourself.

I WENT to Irbil in Iraqi Kurdistan because it was one of few places that someone with a Syrian passport could go without a visa. From there I started a four-month journey. I paid someone to take me to Turkey. My idea was to settle there, feel safe, and then try to get my family out of Lebanon. But when I got to Turkey, my thinking changed completely. I decided to turn to Europe. I told myself, "I don't care. If I have to sell a kidney, I'll do it." There was no other choice. I had nothing else. It was the difference between being and not being.

I met other Syrians who were leaving and we created a group. We made it to Bodrum, which was about twenty kilometers from the Greek island of Kos. We paid and went out at night, hiding as we waited for the smuggler. There was fear and terror. They told us to go down the cliff to the beach, where I saw the dinghy. I didn't get in. I didn't want to drown and was willing to pay more to go on a fishing boat.

The next week we made another attempt with a smuggler. The boat was meant for two or three people, but there were fifteen people and no place to sit. The smuggler pointed a gun at me and said, "Get on." I told him, "I'm Syrian. I've seen worse than the weapon in your hand. I will stand here and scream. The authorities will return me to Syria, but you'll be charged as a smuggler and go to jail."

The third time I was introduced to another smuggler who was more honest. We got on a bigger boat. The trip took fifty minutes.

◉

IN KOS, the first hotel kicked me out. I kept thinking, "Who's going to catch me now? If they catch me, they'll beat me and send me back." You can't even imagine the terror until I reached a hotel that took me in. During all that time, I had no idea what was happening. I didn't know where I was going or what would happen to me.

In Athens, we went from smuggler to smuggler, from one bad person to another. I tried to leave from the airport on a forged European ID, like millions of other refugees. Over forty days, I made four attempts. On the fifth time, I made it.

During those forty days in Greece, I read about the history of the Netherlands. I learned that the Netherlands provided more freedom than anywhere else in Europe. I'd experienced oppression and fear and not being able to speak. The Netherlands was where I wanted to go. People shared information on YouTube and Facebook. I learned that the population of the Netherlands was seventeen million. I knew every household had four or five bicycles. I memorized the provinces and their borders.

When I arrived at the Rotterdam airport, I knew to go to an area called Ter Apel to turn myself in. I reached the refugee shelter but couldn't find the front door. A police car passed me but didn't pay too much attention. After a while, the same car stopped and a cop came out. I got scared. We think that all police are like *our* police. That's burned into our brains. It's instinctual, involuntary.

The officer came up to me with a wide smile and said in English, "I can tell you're lost. How can I help you?" He didn't ask for my passport or my ID. He didn't ask my nationality or language or religion or anything else. He said, "What do you need?'

I said, "I can't find the door of the shelter."

He said, "I'll walk you there."

He was very gentle. Even the tone of his voice was soft. There was calmness in the way he walked. He knew what he was doing. He left a safe space between us—a space that creates feelings of trust, not fear. Someone else might not have noticed that space, but I did.

He took me to the door and said, "Do you need help with anything else?" He saw that my hand was shaking and that I wasn't acting normally. He said, "Is someone pressuring you? Is someone hurting you?"

I told him, "No. I'm just Syrian."

Manaf

JORDAN

We moved to Jordan. I found work at a pastry shop to support our family. I wasn't studying or building my future. And I wasn't saving because I gave seventy to eighty percent of my salary to my parents. I had a bad manager and bad coworkers who talked about me behind my back. I worked sixty hours a week and it gave me a back injury that I've now spent years working with a chiropractor to fix.

One day, I received a phone call from Syria. It lasted less than two minutes, but it changed my life. It was from a guy named Ghiath, who's someone I'd met at university. I think a mutual friend must have mentioned me and he got my number just to say hi. I asked him how he was doing. He said, "Well, I'm managing." I asked him, "How's the university?" He said, "I can't go. I'm wanted." I had an immediate reaction. My parents always told us to stay away from politics. I didn't ask him any further questions.

Apparently, this guy was with some group considered to be terrorists. I had no idea. The next day I received a call from someone who said he was from Jordanian intelligence. At that time, Syrians sometimes pranked each other with those types of calls. I told him, "I'm sorry, but can I verify that this is for real?" I gave the phone to my Jordanian coworker, and the man told him, "Call this number for Jordanian intelligence and tell them to transfer you to this office." We did that, and the same man picked up. "Hello," he said. "It's me. Is it verified now?" I looked at my coworker, like "What do I do?" He said, "If they call, you go. You don't mess with the government."

☺

I WENT to the intelligence complex. You wait for two to four hours. They take you from building to building on buses with closed curtains so you can't see anything.

Eventually I got to an office. There the man didn't even say hello before he asked, "Who is Ghiath?" He put a file on the desk and told me, "I want to check your phone." He checked my messages and calls and every app. He kept asking me to tell him everything. Finally, he said, "I want you to contact Ghiath and bring me information."

I said, "Information about what?"

He said, "Where he is. What he's doing. Everything."

I had no choice. He could have sent my family home.

I think the intelligence officer called me another two or three times. I gave him very small answers, and I guess he got bored because he stopped calling after that. I figured I was safe.

☺

TIME WENT by. Syrians and others started taking those boats from Turkey to Greece. I wanted to do that too. I had a group of friends and we all wanted a better future. Our aim was Germany. I started planning. My mom sold a couple of gold rings. I tried to teach myself some German words online. I was ready. I booked a flight to Turkey.

I went to the airport in Amman and passed through all the steps. A guy was literally about to put an exit stamp in my passport when he checked my name and asked, "Have you ever been contacted by Jordanian intelligence? There will be no flight today. Please visit us again at the same office where you visited before."

After the weekend, I went back to the intelligence office and went through the whole process a second time. The waiting, the stress. I sat there, looking at the same guy who had interrogated me six months earlier. He said, "Don't bother booking another ticket, you'll just lose it. We'll call you and let you know when you may leave."

℗

I WENT back to my bad job at the pastry shop. One day, my dad saw some Facebook post about the British Council offering a free one-hundred-hour English language course. My dad wanted me to apply. I really saw no future in this. What was the point? I was already working sixty hours a week.

I didn't want to do it, so I missed the deadline. But not enough people applied, and they extended the deadline. My dad kept giving me such a headache about it. I didn't want to argue with him, so I said, "Okay, fine."

At the British Council, a guy named John was the teacher. He was super cool. The one hundred hours passed, and John said that there was a free exam that I could take. I'd get a certificate that was useless, but a nice memento. Later, John called to invite me to take another language test. And then another time, they called me to attend an event. I wasn't really invested in it, but the transport money motivated me. They offered to pay for transportation from the town where I was living to the capital, which would save around ten Jordanian dinars.

After the event, everyone was sitting around and eating snacks. I chatted with a young Syrian woman. She told me that she was waiting to travel to Canada. I said, "How did you manage that?" She said that there was a scholarship called "World University Service of Canada." Basically, it was a program to help refugees who weren't able to continue their studies. I'd never heard of it. She said that I should follow them on Facebook and wait for an announcement about applications.

The whole process from when I applied to when I left for Canada took fifteen months. I remember when I read that I would be going to Saskatchewan. I didn't even know how to pronounce it.

Medea

CAIRO, EGYPT

My mom, five sisters, and I started packing to leave from Damascus to Egypt. We said, "Two months and then we'll come back home." I remember that I called a friend who had already left Syria. He told me, "Don't listen to them. You're not coming back. Pack whatever you want for the rest of your life." I filled my bag with art stuff. I packed the drawing paper that my dad had given me when we used to draw together, before he passed away. I packed his pens and pencils and the book that we used to read together.

My mother got frustrated, like she was giving up. She said, "Why are you packing this? Take useful things!" This is something that someone not into art would say. People who don't draw don't understand that this is your escape. I was packing my own shelter, my pain reliever. I packed stuff to remind myself of who I am. Maybe someday if I forgot where I came from, I would be able to look at it and say, "I used to belong there."

The week that we packed was horrible. It was like the country telling you: "Go out. Don't miss me." Our neighborhood had no electricity and no water. No stores were open and there was nothing to buy. We managed to get rice, but it had little bugs inside. Now, I always say that it was both a curse and a blessing. It was a curse because it's like your mother telling you, "I don't want to see you." But a blessing because she is doing that on purpose. She doesn't want you to miss her. She does this so you will be able to leave.

⌒

WE ARRIVED in Egypt and I heard all these people speaking with an Egyptian accent. I felt like I was in some kind of Egyptian soap opera. I thought, "Do you guys speak like this for real? All the time?"

At first, we stayed with relatives. Then we got our own apartment, but it was empty. We couldn't afford beds, only the mattresses. We used cardboard boxes as tables. I made a bunch of drawings and put them on the walls to make it feel like home. It was the drawings that made my room something that belonged to me. Still, we never unpacked our bags completely. Whenever we wanted anything, we'd just take it out of the suitcase. I think this was a sign from God that it was just a temporary place.

My sister and I found work at an NGO. These were the first jobs we'd ever had. I worked as an art facilitator making workshops and safe spaces for children. My family says that I have a childish mind, so working with kids was like playing with friends. I worked with amazing people who knew me before I knew myself. They looked inside my soul and told me things about myself that I only discovered later. People like that are another thing that makes a place home.

It was a good life. Then there was the coup.* Morsi was gone. Sisi came. A lot of awful things happened. They made it hard for Syrian students to enroll in universities. Our hope of going to university one day was demolished.

---

* In 2013, the Egyptian armed forces launched a coup that deposed the Muslim Brotherhood's Mohamed Morsi, the country's first democratically elected president. During Morsi's one year in power, the government allowed Syrians to enter Egypt with only a passport and receive access to public healthcare, education, and food subsidies on par with Egyptians. The subsequent military regime and its supporters accused Syrian refugees of backing the Muslim Brotherhood and abetting terrorism. As the government under Abdel Fattah el-Sisi reinstated entry restrictions, Syrians in Egypt experienced new levels of hate speech, harassment, and arrests, as well as hundreds of cases of forced return to Syria.

We talked to a friend in Istanbul and asked him about universities there. He said, "Send me your papers and I will check on availability." One month later, he told us that we got accepted. We were shocked. My grandpa was against our moving. He told my mom, "Are you crazy? You're six women. How are you going to survive in Turkey on your own?" My mom told him that we had no other option.

We packed our stuff again and said goodbye to our friends in Egypt. On the airplane, I cried my heart out. The flight attendant kept saying, "Please ma'am, calm down." We all felt like we were something in Egypt. We *became* something in Egypt. We were doing something for the community and we were needed. And that is enough to satisfy any human being.

III

SEARCHING

OKBA, FATIMA, SUHEIR, HANI, MAI,

MEHYAR, RIFAIE, MOHAMMED A.,

RAMY, MEDEA, RIMA

Searching for home after displacement is a quest for the elements of security, love, authenticity, fulfillment, and connection that allow one to feel belonging and possibility in a new place. This search often involves a struggle to accept a new environment and is also shaped by the ways in which one is or is not accepted by that environment itself.

The worldwide dispersal of Syrian refugees provides a window into how such searches for home vary greatly depending on where they unfold. For some of the 5.5 million Syrian refugees living in the Middle East, geographic, cultural, and linguistic proximity to their country of origin rekindles some of the familiar warmth of home. Indeed, Turks, Lebanese, and Jordanians often initially welcomed fleeing Syrians as brothers and sisters. As time wore on, however, these local communities increasingly came to insist that they hosted too many Syrians and even called for refugees to leave.

More fundamentally, these states' lack of legal protections for refugees, compounded by their own grave economic crises and the failure of wealthier countries to provide sufficient aid, have created conditions that impede refugees' long-term stability. About 95 percent of displaced Syrians in the countries bordering Syria reside outside formal refugee camps.[1] While they obtain some limited assistance from UN agencies and charitable organizations, most refugee families struggle to pay rent and meet daily expenses. Those who find jobs typically work in the informal sector with low pay and harsh conditions and without legal recourse should employers prove unscrupulous. Among those in exploitative labor markets are hundreds of thousands of refugee children who are not in school.

As of the end of 2023, about 1.5 million Syrians had received asylum in countries in the EU, with 56 percent of them in Germany.[2] Here, the search for home brings different obstacles and opportunities. Many European governments had the means to transform public spaces into shelters to accommodate asylum seekers upon arrival, and thereafter to provide integration courses, job retraining, and other welfare benefits to assist newcomers in building new lives. Still, transitions have been far from easy. Language barriers and state bureaucracy could make asylum seekers' first years in Europe an exasperating maze of paperwork, miscommunication, and waiting. And while countless locals volunteered their time or even their homes to welcome refugees, others responded with veiled suspicion or outright hostility. More generally, many Syrians experienced European society as individualistic and distant, and thus a stark contrast with a sense of home grounded in continuous social contact with family, neighbors, and friends. Creating a home could therefore demand that Syrian newcomers adjusted their notions of what home meant—or that they carved out some private homeplace that went against the cultural grain of the larger milieu.

The narratives in this section show how individuals searching for home navigate this complex terrain. With his plans to reach the Netherlands derailed, Okba finds himself in a small village in Bavaria and struggles to connect with its residents. Fatima, having left her beloved balcony overlooking both demonstrations and burials, adjusts to Amman by obtaining a job for the first time. Suheir discovers love and purpose in a community center for Arab refugees and migrants in Istanbul, but also hits upon a crucial element of home that lies beyond her control: the freedom to come and go from it. Now years after he defected from the army and said goodbye to his comrade Abu Jaber, Hani looks for traces of home in Chicago and also ponders his parents' integration in Turkey. All four speakers offer some comments on how one particular factor affects refugees' searches for home: gender. They recount the stereotype that young men are not deserving refugees, describe how displacement unsettles gendered expectations about employment, offer a window into single mothering in exile, and explore differences in how older men and women respond to being uprooted. The diversity of their observations indicates that there is no single way that gender impacts home-making in exile, but it is an important part of the story.

Other testimonials reveal how opportunity and prejudice influence the search for home. Mai relishes both the kindness and equal protection before the law that she finds in Canada. Mehyar recounts a different experience in Norway, where he is overwhelmed by both natural beauty and everyday Islamophobia. Several narrators spotlight questions of race and ethnicity. Rifaie had never really thought about race until he encounters public discourse in Australia, reads *The Autobiography of Malcolm X*, and asks if he, too, is a person of color. In Sudan, Mohammed A. experiences being regarded as white in a majority Black environment, as well as adjusting to lesser economic development than that to which he is accustomed. Ramy moves to South Africa and finds relief that, in contrast to the other countries where he has attempted to live, he is not pigeonholed by his own origins.

The sum of these stories conveys how searches for home encounter innumerable points of friction between individuals and their environments. But this tension can be beautiful rather than alienating. Though she cried unconsolably when she left Egypt, Medea comes into her own in Turkey, where she adopts a new life and language and learns to appreciate what is novel in her surroundings. Rima develops a special connection to Beirut as she looks for moments of understanding across political divides. Her reflections, like those of others in this section, give expression to both challenge and gratification, and sometimes the gratification of working through the challenge itself. In searching for home in strange lands, people might look for the promise of a fresh start, the smile of a potential friend, the ability to preserve some part of their past, or simply the chance, as Ramy puts it, "to live a normal life." The search for home, in other words, is a search for an end to searching.

Okba

TROGEN, GERMANY

The German police brought us from the train to the police station where they took our fingerprints. There is a law here in Europe: a refugee who gets fingerprints taken in one EU country is not allowed to continue on to another one. So, I couldn't go to the Netherlands. I stayed in Germany. That's the story of how I came here.

They sent me to a refugee camp and then to a small village in northern Bavaria called Trogen. In most German villages there are only old people. Young people move to the big cities. Because there were no children in Trogen anymore, they turned the school into a hotel for refugees. You can imagine how beautiful that situation was for me! I had a warm place and a bed. I had Internet and could call my mother and tell her that everything was fine. I could say that I was in Europe. I didn't have to lie anymore.

I shared a room with another Syrian named Haytham. There were other refugees from Kosovo and Ukraine, but they didn't speak English. After two weeks, it got very boring. I went out for a walk. I couldn't say anything in German, but I said hello to everyone I saw. "Hello! Hello!" I tried to be friendly. "Hello!" Some people answered and others just looked at me like this was very strange. That was hard for me.

Google is the solution for everything, so I searched Google. I threw in the name of the village. Everything was in German, but I used Google to translate. I found email addresses for the village council, two people who worked at the cemetery, and a priest named Father Amarell. I wrote them emails. My English was bad. The translation in German was *very* bad. When I show it to Germans now, they just laugh.

7 February 2015 at 15:01

Hallo Vater Amarell,

Mein name ist Okba Kerdiea.

Vor allem, sorry für mein schlechtes Deutsch Übersetzung weil ich Google, diese Botschaft zu übersetzen. Ich bin syrischen und ich lebe jetzt in der alten Schule in

Eggeten 8

95183 Trogen

mit 9 Personen von Kosova und Okrain. In der Tat, ich dein Dorf sehr gut gefallen. Es ist ruhig und schön. Und die Leute sind so nett und freundlich. Aber es ist ein Problem, ich habe Lust, darüber zu sprechen:

Ich möchte in Ihrer Gemeinde anzuschließen und wirksam sein und den Menschen helfen, und in sinnvolle Arbeit ehrenamtlich. Ich bin allein hier im Hotel weil niemand spricht Englisch, Deutsch und ich nicht weiß, noch. So wünsche ich, wenn ich mit den Menschen hier zu kontaktieren, Freunde, Freiwilligen und anderen zu helfen.

Schließlich danke Ihnen so sehr. Ihnen, Okba

Hello Father Amarell

my name is OKBA Kerdiea.

first of all, sorry for my bad German translation because I used Google to translate this message. I am Syrian and I live now in the old school in

Eggeten 8

95183 Trogen

with 9 people from Kosova and Okrain. in fact, I liked your village very much. it's quiet and beautiful. and people are so kind and friendly. but there is an issue I would like to talk about:

I would like to join in your community and be effective and help people and to volunteer in useful work. I'm alone here in the hotel, because nobody speaks English, and I dont know German yet. so I wish if I can contact with the people here, make friends, volunteer and help others. finally, thank you so much.

yours, OKBA

A few days passed, and I received no answer from the church, city hall, or cemetery. I thought that if I wanted to get to know people, I should go to the church on Sunday. Then I could meet Father Amarell too.

On Sunday, I took Haytham and went. I was very shy. All these elderly people went to church and saw two strangers—refugees!—just walking around, shyly. They looked at us and whispered. I thought that maybe I shouldn't go inside the church. Instead, we just walked around for two hours until the service finished and people started to come out again.

I decided that I needed to be a little brave, so I said, "Hello! Do you speak English?"

Everyone stared. One said, "A little."

"May I talk to Father Amarell?"

All the answers came in German. I didn't see a single smile. Maybe they thought that I was coming to beg for money? I told Haytham, "Let's go home." I felt very bad. I thought, "Why the hell did I come to Germany? I should have gone to the Netherlands."

The next week, I went back to the church. The same thing happened. I was too shy to go inside, so we waited outside. When they finished, I asked again, "Hello, do you speak English?" One lady said yes. And then before I could say anything else, she said, "Are you living in the refugee home?"

I said, "Yes."

She asked, "How many people are there? Are there women or children?"

I said, "We are nine people and there are no women or children."

Then she left. Why didn't she ask me about what I wanted? I didn't want help. I just wanted to connect with people. I told Haytham, "I will never contact another person. I will never say hello. I will never greet anyone again."

Fatima

AMMAN, JORDAN

Our house in Syria wasn't just a home. It was something left to us by my father, who bought it before he died. I have every corner and every detail of that house memorized by heart. I felt connected even to the particles of dust. Sometimes when I walked to school, I took one route. The next time, I took a different route. That way, I thought, I would definitely put my foot where my father had stepped.

At the same time, the house overlooked the cemetery, where you could find everyone you loved. Here lie my great-grandmother, my grandfather, my cousin. Over there is my father's grave. I felt that I was in an earthly life overlooking heavenly life.

I came to Jordan hating everyone and everything. I couldn't stand it. I couldn't grasp what had happened. I looked with disgust at anyone wearing a police or army uniform. I couldn't breathe. I felt strangled, suffocating, as if there was no oxygen. I was thirsty but didn't want to drink their water. I'd wake up and weep. I wanted to return.

My mother finally got really angry at me and yelled, "What can I do? We're not going back! You must accept this new life."

@

WE WERE considered to be a wealthy family, but all our wealth was in land and properties. We didn't have any savings, any cash. In Jordan, we all tried to cut costs and eat as little as possible. My paternal uncles and brother refused to work in degrading jobs. My family is conservative and against women working. But when my maternal uncle started to work at a tissue factory, I decided to work there too. My family agreed.

In the factory, you had to work like a machine, packing tissues in boxes. If I stopped to adjust my shawl, they'd glare at me like I was wasting time. I couldn't understand how people were expected to work like this. I couldn't understand how I, a college graduate, was working in a factory with people who'd never finished school. There was this girl who was mean to me and sped up the conveyor belt so it was impossible for me to catch up. I managed to pack the first three tissues quickly, but the fourth fell on the floor.

I isolated myself in my own world, listening to the song "Syria, My Beloved" on my headphones when I worked. *Syria, my beloved, you restored my dignity.* That's all I listened to. I had it on replay and listened to the same song again and again. Thousands of times, for hours. I didn't want to hear anything but that song. Maybe I wanted to feel like I was still in Syria. Sometimes the music energized me and I worked faster, and sometimes it made me feel rebellious. I remember once writing "Syria, My Beloved" on the wall in the break room.

They deducted ten dinars from my paycheck for that. And they deducted more when I dropped the tissues on the floor. But when I got my own wages for the first time, I bought a small mobile phone. That was a big achievement for me.

◎

WORKING IN the tissue factory was very degrading, but I was still upset with myself when I quit. I thought maybe I should have been more humble. Then I heard that there were jobs with a Syrian organization doing work at Akilah Hospital, where they brought the injured from Syria for treatment. I started working there. My job was to prepare spreadsheets listing the equipment used and write descriptions about patients' cases to post on the organization's Facebook page.

In the beginning, I was happy. The patients and I consoled each other. At that point, if you told me that you are Syrian, I would immediately love you with all my heart.

It was the first time I saw severely wounded people. One patient was named Dalal. She had been hit by a missile and had a hole in her leg where the bone showed through. Her four-year-old daughter died in her arms but she was in denial and was convinced that she'd never had a daughter in the first place. Another patient was a revolutionary activist. The regime tortured her to the extent that she became paralyzed. She was extremely thin, and her arms seemed as if they were melting, fused into the bed. I saw her as a melted jasmine flower, laying there under a white bedsheet. I cried whenever I saw her, and she would tell me, "I'm strong! You should be strong too."

Suheir

My son Mohammed was fourteen and Syrian security forces were starting to kidnap kids his age. My ex-husband was in France, and I told him that I wanted to send Mohammed to him. He decided that we should apply for a visa from the consulate in Turkey because he knew someone there who could help process it.

We traveled to Istanbul. Mohammed got the visa and flew to his father. I'd come to Turkey with only a small bag, not even a suitcase. Then the bombing and shelling intensified back home. My brother was detained. I couldn't go back.

I stayed in Istanbul, and the months went by. I met a guy who was very outgoing and always invited me to different events. Once, he invited me to a lecture on journalism during the Syrian revolution. My housemate at the time was one of these people who saw everything in a negative light. She said, "Don't go. Those people are just using Syrians to raise money."

I thought that she might be right, but decided to go anyway. There I met two people, one of whom later became a good friend. A friend of his was establishing a community center for the Arab diaspora and refugees called "Ad-Dar." Ad-Dar means "house" or "home" in Arabic. The first event held at Ad-Dar was a poetry reading, and I attended.

I GOT my Turkish residency permit. I needed income and found work cleaning houses and offices. The job was completely unrelated to my education or professional experience. But I wanted to ensure that I didn't rely on anyone for help.

Mohammed was in France for two months when my ex-husband sent him back, saying that he should stay with me until his French residency was finalized. Otherwise, his visa in France would expire and his stay in France would be illegal. Once Mohammed got back to Turkey, my ex-husband sent me an email: "Keep the kid. I don't want him."

Returning to Syria was no longer an option. My priority was my son's safety. I feared that he could get detained and I'd lose him forever. So, I decided to stay in Turkey. I became like the millions of other people living here.

Mohammed was depressed and sitting at home all the time. I thought about Ad-Dar. It would give him a chance to make friends, so he joined Ad-Dar as a volunteer. Ad-Dar also had a scholarship program to teach students the skills they needed to apply to schools. I enrolled Mohammed because I wanted him to keep busy with something productive and meaningful.

Not long after that, a staff member at Ad-Dar took a different job and her position became vacant. Though my job at the time paid more, I quit and started to work at Ad-Dar full time. At first, it was only a job for me. With time, it stopped feeling like work. Going to Ad-Dar became like seeing family. I became very attached to it, emotionally. How can I describe it? Work ended at three o'clock in the afternoon, but I'd stay until nine. I was doing everything: welcoming people, organizing activities, coordinating the women's knitting project. People came for language courses. Every Friday, families gathered to watch movies. Every Saturday, we hosted a kitchen club and made a dish from a different hometown. I'd cook for an endless number of people. It made me so happy to watch people eating something delicious. The center attracted volunteers from around the world and I made friends from many countries. There were people who needed me and people I needed too.

⟨©⟩

MEANWHILE, I applied to the UN for us to be resettled as refugees. Our top choice for relocation was the United States. The UN regarded the fact that I'm a single mother as an urgent case. They called it a "woman exposed to danger." That helped expedite the process. It actually went quickly: everything was done and we were just waiting to schedule our flights. But the file suddenly stalled.

During that same period, my son earned a full scholarship to study in the US. He traveled to the US on a student visa, and I stayed behind, hoping that I'd follow soon. Then Trump became president. My resettlement application was denied, and I got stuck in Istanbul. I stayed behind and let him go forward and have a better life. Everything I do is for him to have opportunity in the future.

⟨©⟩

MOHAMMED FINISHED high school and earned a scholarship for college. And then, he was diagnosed with bipolar disorder. I fell apart. That was the moment when I came to experience real unfairness. My son needed my care more than ever before. He had no family in the US or barely anyone to stay with. Maybe one hug from his mother could help alleviate his pain. But I wasn't even allowed to apply for a visa to travel to him, simply because I have a Syrian passport. Being Syrian made me a criminal for a crime that I didn't commit.

If my son hadn't become sick, I'd be very happy living in Istanbul. It's a charming city, filled with life. The buildings and streets remind me of Damascus, where the streets have soul. I feel like I belong to this place, but I'm not attached. If it's in my best interest to move, I'll move and create the same environment for myself somewhere else.

My needs are simple, and they're being met here. The only problem is not having paperwork to travel to be with my son. I didn't have the papers to go back to Syria to be with my mom when she was dying either. This is what has hurt me more than anything else. I lived through the horrors of the war in Syria, but never experienced the injustice of being Syrian until I wasn't allowed to travel. During Mohammed's most difficult moments, I'm the only person in the world he trusts. The only way for us to communicate is by phone. Afternoon for him in the US is the middle of the night for me in Turkey, so I started staying up late and experiencing sleeping disorders. Sometimes I open video calls with him, and we don't even talk. We're just relieved to see each other. The real depression starts when the call ends.

Hani

CHICAGO, USA

Whan I see how homeless people are treated here in Chicago, it reminds me of when I was with the armed group in Deir ez-Zor and how people in the area viewed us. People want to help homeless people, but don't want them near their homes. They want them five blocks away.

There is a lot of work that we need to do, myself or whoever moves into a new community. We owe something to the people who welcomed us. But they also have to understand and have respect. Know that refugees didn't want to come here. Refugees left everything and came to a city that doesn't look like them. With people who don't look like them. Where everything is different. They don't speak the language. They don't belong to the culture. And, still, the expectation is that they become part of the community.

There will always be some reminder that you're not from here. Like today, actually, I went to buy lentils from the grocery store. The guy didn't understand my accent. He said, "What do you want?"

I said, "Lentils."

He said, "What is that?"

I said, "Lentils. You know, lentils. Red lentils, brown lentils. It's like a grain."

He said, "I don't understand what you're saying." He grabbed somebody else. And the other guy said, "What do you mean? Say that again?"

It took them like five minutes to understand. Finally, I thought, "You know what? I don't want lentils from you." And I walked out and went to the Arab grocery store.

෧

POSSIBLY THE cruelest thing that Assad did to us was that he made us all irrelevant. If you remove people from their context and put them where nobody knows them, they become irrelevant. Even after a few years here, I'm nobody. I don't know anyone or anything. I don't know the streets. I'm not in a community.

We're irrelevant in communities that don't welcome us. We're millions of obsolete people in different parts of the world. That's why people live in the bubble of the small communities that they make in Chicago or Berlin or France. They become relevant in that bubble. They become a person. Once you take them outside that bubble, they're no one.

Like my dad. He was the head of the family. We owned thousands of acres. People consulted him. Nothing happened in my entire extended family without him consenting to it. If you had offered my dad a pot of gold to move from Deir ez-Zor to Damascus he would have refused, because Deir ez-Zor was his home and his whole life.

Now my dad is in Turkey and he's so obsolete. He's nobody. He hates it, but he doesn't want to say that. Instead, he says, "I want to go back home." Every day he calls me and is like, "We want to buy olive trees and plant them in the farm." And I'm like, "What farm, Dad? What are you talking about?"

Men are the weakest part of Syrian society. My dad gave up from day one in Turkey. Now he lives on memories. But my mom is incredible. She made a community for herself. She is learning Turkish. Okay, she's seventy and isn't really going to learn Turkish, but she's trying. She has a notebook and writes down words.

෧

ONCE, WHEN my family was still in Syria, the army was doing raids. I was in Turkey then and lost touch with them for three days. We received news that people were getting killed. I took a bus to the border, crossed, and went immediately to Deir ez-Zor. I couldn't think about anything else. I was on the way when I got a phone call: "Your family is safe and went to the farm."

We have a farmhouse but it's not really suitable to live in. It's just one room. I got there and stayed with them on the farm for a long time. After a while, my mom said, "I'm going to travel back home to Deir ez-Zor to get some plates."

I was like, "Come on, I can buy new plates. Why do you need to go?"

You know, *my* plates. "My forks, my knives, my house. I need to get them."

She went. She took a boat to cross the river into territory under government control. Take a cab, go home, pick up stuff, take another cab, cross the river again, and you're back in opposition-held territory. She came back and was like, "See? It's fine. I can do it."

She did that a few times. Then it started to become really dangerous. The army positioned a sniper at the checkpoint and killed some people.

After a few days, my mom said, "I want to go back to the house."

I said, "Now it's actually dangerous. You shouldn't go."

We fought about it for two days. I said, "What are you going to get?"

And she said, "A few things. I have a list of stuff."

"Can I see the list?"

"No."

My mom was going, and I couldn't stop it. She took a woman who worked on the farm, and they crossed together. On the way there, the sniper opened fire. If he'd wanted, he could have shot them. But he sort of shot around them instead. On the way back, shells landed in the river. One of the boats capsized, but their boat did not. She was very lucky.

We got back to the farm, and she had one of those huge duffle bags. A very heavy bag. I was like, "What did you go for? I want to see what you got."

And she had brought photographs. All the family photographs. I went and had a moment by myself. I thought, "Thank you."

My dad would never do that. He would say, "Forget the pictures. I don't want to die." I think that women in our culture understand the meaning of these kinds of details. The importance of preserving our history. If we lose our pictures, we lose our history. That's what was happening to everybody else. My mom saw that and she acted.

Mai

MISSISSAUGA, CANADA

I never imagined that I'd love Canada as much as I do. I'm known among my friends for that. If anyone arrives here and doesn't like how things are, they send them to me.

What is most important to me here is security. I feel secure in all meanings of the word. I can walk down the street in the middle of the night. And in Canada, we've tasted the sweetness of the law. Law shapes people. In Syria, there was a guy who shot his wife right in front of her mother. You know how long he stayed in prison? Two months. Why? Because he paid off the judge. In Syria, money settles everything. You can take the noose off a man's neck by paying a bribe. Compare that to Canada, where you feel that the law is there to protect you and others. If you respect the law, then everyone must respect you.

There are no nicer people than Canadians. I've never met anyone who is racist or talked to me rudely. At first, I never spoke because I was embarrassed to make mistakes in English. But they encourage you. They help, saying, "Oh, do you mean this? Are you trying to say that?" Sometimes I'll be driving and make a horrible mistake and think, "Oh no, they're going to honk and yell at me!" And then you look over and find someone smiling and saying, "Are you okay?"

I hope people here stay like this. Sometimes I tell my husband, "God protect Canada from us Syrians and the mentality that we carry with us."

꩜

THEY CALL Mississauga "Arabssauga." There's a big Arab population. Anywhere you go, there are Arabs. You go to Arab stores. At the bank there are Arab receptionists.

So many of the people who make it here from Syria and the Middle East have amazing work experience. There are doctors, pharmacists . . . but they encounter huge obstacles. They have to go back and study from scratch and pay a lot of money to get their diplomas recognized. My husband used to be deputy director of a medical company selling open-heart equipment. He speaks English well and has twenty-five years of work experience. He keeps sending his CV to places, but not a single company has even offered him an interview because he doesn't have *Canadian* experience. Now he's working for Uber Eats so we can pay the bills. Everyone around us is working for Uber Eats or as a laborer. There are doctors working at Tim Hortons.

Thank God, we're better off than most. Three-quarters of the people from my hometown in Syria are now living in refugee camps. There's going to be an entire generation of kids without education and even a semblance of hope. May God help them. We say, "Thank God, we're better off than most."

Mehyar

OSLO, NORWAY

My parents are Palestinian refugees.* We were poor when I was a child. And then everyone in the family worked and we became middle-class. I was twenty-seven and I had a girlfriend who was the love of my life. Your life is on track and then, suddenly, everything evaporates. You end up in exile. You're in a white country and you're not white. You have to learn a new language. You have to prove that you're good enough. You have to prove that you're innocent. That you're a victim, not a potential terrorist.

I came to Norway and was transferred to a little village in the middle of the country. It was culture shock to go from Damascus to a place with a magical nature. There was a peaceful fjord. The sea penetrates tens of kilometers deep into the land. My first impression was, "What the hell is all this beauty?" It's an overwhelming kind of beauty. It was more than I could take.

I started to discover that people in the village have a lot of stereotypes about people who look like me. I began my personal battle to prove, "I'm as good as you are. I'm equal to you." This battle caused me stress and the stress developed into anxiety. I'd experienced depression

---

* The 1948 war that established the state of Israel led to the expulsion or forced flight of an estimated 750,000 Palestinians as refugees. Some 90,000 resettled in Syria. This, along with later waves of displacement, brought the population of registered Palestinian refugees in Syria to 527,000 by 2011.

before, but I didn't even understand the word "anxiety." To be sad is one thing. To be afraid of your own thoughts is something else.

People develop anxiety when they think about the future all the time. I'd spent all the money I'd saved when we were moving from one place to another in Damascus. Then I had to borrow money for my travel and my brother's travel. Smuggling yourself is really expensive. It cost like fifteen thousand euros to travel from Syria to Norway. When I got here, I was obsessed with getting a job as soon as possible. And in that small village in the middle of the country, there were no opportunities, not even for locals.

I eventually got a job teaching math to new students with Arab backgrounds. My main goal was to make them feel safe in this new environment. The huge majority were traumatized. I also started doing some voluntary activities with the Red Cross. Later, I heard that a neighboring village needed an Arabic speaker to work as an assistant in a school. I took that job and then got a job in another school. And then got a job at a supermarket and a nursing home. I took all the jobs that were available and always had two jobs at the same time.

Sometimes people gave me looks. Sometimes things happened. I remember one day I was working at the school and forgot some papers in my bag in my office. I went back to my office and found one of my colleagues searching my bag. He saw me coming and was very embarrassed. I never asked him about it, and he never told me.

I discovered that Islam is much more important in Norway than it is in Syria. One evening I was at the cash register at the supermarket and an old lady said in Norwegian, "I'm Christian, I believe in Jesus. Are you a Muslim?" I looked at her and said, "You know what, I'm not Muslim. I don't even like God. I don't think God is a very good guy."

When Norwegians get drunk, they start asking you very strange questions. "Are you Muslim? Have you ever been a Muslim? What do you think about Muslims? What do you think about Islam?" If you're not a Muslim, then you score more points. If you drink alcohol, you're even better. If you eat pork, then you're open-minded and a wonderful human being.

I've never been obsessed with religion the way I am now. I found myself defending Muslims, even though I don't care about religion. My mother is very religious, but in Syria it was okay if you chose another path. Here, you're a Muslim regardless of how you define yourself. Any dark person is Muslim, and Muslims are horrible. They bring terrorism to our country. They have a lot of kids who will take over our continent.

I think the West is very unsafe for people who look like me. For three years, I was treated like a trashy person. It was all-consuming. When you're busy proving yourself, you stop genuinely developing. I reached the point that I was fed up.

◎

HAVE YOU ever experienced forgetting who you are? I don't know how to describe it. It's like you have something precious inside you and then you're emptied. You feel like you have nothing to offer anyone anymore, not even feelings.

When I moved from the village to Oslo, I didn't know if I was full of hate or full of anger. I didn't want to get to know anybody, especially ethnic Norwegians. In Syria, we're very dependent on each other and you're always surrounded by people. In Norway, the easiest thing is to be alone. Even in the middle of a very crowded city, you're totally alone.

Things eventually got better. If I'd lived my whole life in the village, I'd hate the entire West. But I saved myself here in Oslo. I made friends from Norway and all over the world. I began to remember who I was and the values that I was raised on and am proud of.

Recently, my Norwegian friends and I took a trip to Jordan. It was wonderful. I never really appreciated the sun in Syria because we had it all the time. In Jordan, I was under the sun again and feeling its energy. We went to the desert, and the horizon was endless. I can't say that I felt like I was back home, but it was the only day in more than five years that I wasn't anxious. My friends said, "We've never seen you like this before."

At the same time, I observed the corruption from the moment I landed in the airport. I remembered that Damascus was also a place of horrible corruption. For someone like me, who was forced to leave, it was very necessary to remember Damascus for the way it was. I started to get beyond the nostalgia. It reminded me of a story I once read about a man who was born blind and then was brought to sight. When he saw for the first time, he was horrified and wanted to go back to blindness. It's the same thing that happens with people who romanticize their homelands. Nostalgia destroys your brain, convincing you that you used to live in heaven. But Syria wasn't heaven. It was just like any other place with advantages and disadvantages.

Home is not always easy to identify, especially once you've experienced exile. In Oslo, I miss Damascus. If I ever visited Damascus again, I reckon that I would miss Oslo. Edward Said once described the exile's condition as a mind of winter. It's very foggy. Home becomes homes.

Rifaie

My dad and brother were killed by the Assad regime. I remember thinking that I needed to stay alive for my mom and little sister. I was an internally displaced person for a month and a half and then went illegally to Turkey. I found work and brought my mom and little sister to come live with me.

It was such a beautiful time. We lived together in one small apartment and developed a unique family union. I played the role of the dad in the family, carrying a lot of responsibilities. I was like a father figure to my sister, who called me "Dad" a couple of times. I told her, "Look, don't call me that. You're old enough to know that I'm your brother, not your dad."

Still, I didn't feel stable in Turkey. My residency was tied to my work. Whenever a job finished, I no longer had a permit. There was a lot of rhetoric against Syrians. They might get kicked out any day if there was a change of government. We needed to start thinking of a stable place that could take all of us: my mom, my sister, and me. Any country where there was a possibility of building a life and where you wouldn't get kicked out. I started applying to universities. Because the visa came first from Australia, I came here.

IN GENERAL, Australians are very easygoing and very friendly. Many of them say hi even when they don't know you.

There's also Islamophobia and xenophobia, and a movement against refugees. Obviously, I've faced issues. I remember once when I was at the library. A white woman opened the wrong locker by mistake and accused me of stealing her things. She said, "Give them to me right now. I can smell a rat when I see one." She called me a rat. A rat! Why was that woman afraid? Because I look different? The memory of that whole experience and the reaction of the library staff was traumatizing for me. Being called a thief. The feeling of injustice. The humiliation.

ONE THING that I've become increasingly aware of in Australia is race. Race is something that gets a lot of attention and political debate here. When my wife and I go out for a walk, we get stares because of how different we look. She's a white Australian, I'm not. I think that, most of the time, people are just curious.

Never in my life had I thought of describing someone as white or whatever. I used to be one of those people who said, "We are all humans." I thought that using terms like race were divisive. But the more time I spent here, the more I started to see, "Oh, this or that actually has something to do with the way I look." Race became a way to convey experiences and share experiences. I became more aware of the concept of "people of color." I had never associated myself with that concept before. Now I do. The more I listened, the more I thought, "That makes sense."

A turning point in my life was reading *The Autobiography of Malcolm X*. It was actually a gift from one of the people of color I met here. And that single book literally changed my way of looking at things. I remember taking a lot of notes. I read it and remembered Syria. I could relate to the oppression, the intolerance, the suffering. I thought, what can we learn from this for Syria and the Syrian cause?

One lesson I learned was hope. He was just one person and he was able to create positive change. If one person can do this, then who knows what other people can do. Another lesson was how long it took. There were incremental gains along the way, but the problems are still not solved today. This reminds me that the ongoing struggle for Syria will continue. I think it's important to think long-term. We're not working for ourselves and maybe not even for our children, but for our grandchildren. Maybe the biggest thing I can do is keep the memory of the revolution alive for my future kids. The biggest disaster would be if they had no connection to Syria.

I SUBMITTED two applications to resettle my mom and sister in Australia. The first application was rejected after three or four years. The second application was sitting there for nearly one and a half years, and all I got was a letter acknowledging receipt. Even lawyers who work in the system know that chances of resettlement are very low—a hundred thousand apply and only a few thousand get it. And they just didn't see our case as urgent.

Whenever I'd go to different places in Australia, I would always send photos to my mom in Turkey and say "*Inshallah*, God willing, you'll come here one day, Mama." In the beginning, I was very hopeful. After the first resettlement application was rejected, I was no longer hopeful. I didn't want my mom to have false hope and then be disappointed. I continued to send her pictures everywhere I went. "I'm here, *Inshallah*, one day you'll come and see it." I'd say it with a smile. But I was just saying the words.

Mohammed A.

KHARTOUM, SUDAN

My culture shock began at the Khartoum airport. There was no air conditioning. My bag was lost. There was no security, you just walked right through. It was totally dark, like a horror movie. After the sun set, the whole city was completely dark.

My mother's friend, Mrs. Mona, met me and took me to the room that she'd rented for me. We went through the streets of Khartoum. I saw only sand and soil. I thought, "Where is the pavement, the sidewalks?"

We reached the room. I opened the door, and it was extremely hot. Like over one hundred degrees, and this was at midnight. Mrs. Mona introduced me to the space: "This is your room. This is your bed."

She gave me a SIM card and said, "Here, you have the package for Golden Internet."

I asked, "So I can make phone calls?"

She said, "Don't worry."

I was all sweaty. I asked her, "What about the air conditioner?"

She pointed, "There it is." I looked at the air conditioner. It's one of those that they use in the desert. It doesn't actually give you cool air. It just takes hot air from outside and recycles it with a bit of humidity and then sprays it in your face.

I started to feel the consequences of my decision. I didn't want to call my parents and upset them, so I called my best friend. "Dude," I told him, "I'm in a bad situation."

"How bad is it?"

"Very bad."

I started explaining things. All the time, I kept sweating because of the heat. We'd spoken for maybe ten minutes, and then: Beep, beep, beep. I looked at the phone. What happened? There was no Internet connection. "The package you purchased has finished."

I said, "No, that can't be true!"

I called Mrs. Mona. "All I did was make one phone call," I said.

"Well, it's only twenty-five megabytes," she told me.

"That's the Golden package?" I said, "twenty-five megabytes?"

⊙

I'M GRATEFUL to Mrs. Mona. I wanted to choose the easy way, using the privilege of the money of a foreigner. I was stereotyping Africa. So cool, I'm going to Africa! I will study there, but also volunteer. I will take pictures with Black kids! It'll be fun, and I'll write in my journal, "I was in Africa, and it was so inspiring."

I realized this wasn't a joke. Mrs. Mona was tough with me. She taught me not to be spoiled. She wanted me to live like local Sudanese. She told me, "I will not let you use expensive transportation." When I say, "expensive transportation," you'll think of a luxury air-conditioned Uber. Trust me, in Sudan expensive transportation is a super-old Soviet taxi. Still, Mrs. Mona wanted me to use buses. One bus after another after another until you reach your destination.

"Expensive transportation is for spoiled people," Mrs. Mona said. "Don't use it. Take buses."

The last bus model in Sudan was produced in 1955 or something. You get on the bus and feel it jiggling like a glass of wine. Once when I was on the bus, I was feeling so sad about my life. I lay my head on the window. It was hot. I just wanted to go back home. I was listening to a sad song that goes, "The trip has ended." I leaned my head on the window and was thinking, "The trip has ended."

And then a car scraped against the bus. It barely touched it. And the whole side of the bus fell off. My head was against the window and, all of a sudden, I'm looking down on the road.

The driver got out, lifted the side of the bus, mended it back on, and we carried on. I asked the woman next to me, "Is this normal?" She was like, "Just relax, you spoiled white boy. It will be fine."

Ramy

JOHANNESBURG, SOUTH AFRICA

"Where are you from?" All my decisions and interactions have been based on not wanting to be asked that question. If people are going to ask me where I'm from, and judge me based on where I'm from, then I don't want to deal with these people. I'm not going to stay in that place.

It began when I went to Lebanon. "Where are you from?" "I'm from Syria." And then I have to start the whole journey of proving that I'm a normal human being. That I'm liberal and open-minded. That I'm educated and from a decent family. That I don't steal, don't kill people, am not a bad person. You can take that journey with some people. With others, you can't even start. They shut you out immediately if you are from *that* place.

In Lebanon, I was always treated like a second-class citizen—that is, a second-class noncitizen. When I first arrived in Jordan, they actually jailed me at the airport along with other Syrians on the plane who were fleeing Lebanon for Jordan. Then Jordan announced that they wanted to reduce the number of Syrians working in the telecommunications sector, so I had to leave Jordan. I was working for an international company, and they gave me two choices: Turkey or South Africa.

I chose South Africa because there are no Syrians here. Literally, no Syrians. Nobody here asks me, "Where are you from?" And if they ask, they won't even recognize Syria as an answer. That's why I chose this place. It's really one hundred percent the reason why I'm here.

I used to love South Africa. Then, things started to get more difficult because of the corruption and crime. The unemployment rate is
the highest in the world. After two years, I thought: I should really start
a family, and this is not the right environment for that.

I secured a job with my company in Germany, where my brother
was. I applied for a visa and got it, which is a dream for most Syrians. I
traveled to Germany but was shocked by the level of racism. I wasn't just
second-class, I was third-class. People said things like, "What are you
doing here? Go back to your country. Do you want to go to the mosque?
Do you want to eat halal meat or something?" When I was looking for
an apartment, I got rejected a few times because they doubted that I
would pay the rent or be a good neighbor. Once a lady sat next to me
on the subway and started to scream at me, saying "dog" and other bad
words I was able to recognize.

These are things that I never experienced in South Africa. So, after
six months, I decided to come back. It was an emotional decision and,
to be honest, I now regret it. South Africa won't ever give me the security of a strong passport. It's not a place where I can grow my career. But
they don't care where I'm from. They just don't care. And that gives me
a very good feeling. It's not a feeling of home. The feeling of home that
I had in Syria before 2011 is gone. I've never felt it again. But here I feel
like a normal human being. And that's very important.

Medea

ISTANBUL, TURKEY

Before my mother and sisters and I left Syria, we didn't know how to work. We didn't know how to express ourselves. We didn't know who we were. That's why God sent us all the way to Egypt to gain experience in how to fight in life. When we came to Turkey, it was easier for us to shift to finding work. After we arrived, friends of friends helped us. Someone translated for us, someone helped us find a home, someone helped us find furniture. It was like we were in the hands of God.

I found work as a cashier in a pastry shop while I studied Turkish. After two years, I knew all the grammar but couldn't speak. It felt like being on mute. It was the first time in my life that I'd experienced that feeling.

My sister found a Turkish association that gave courses about communication, life-coaching, and stuff like that. I said, "Why not? Let's give it a try." In the course, people were crying because the trainer was saying such deep things about knowing your life purpose. I was crying because I didn't understand anything!

Eventually, I decided that I wanted to be a trainer too. Imagine: a trainer who doesn't speak Turkish and is trying to teach in Turkish! I remember one time we were five trainers giving a presentation. My part was in the middle of the presentation. The man giving feedback said, "The presentation was terrific! Especially the standup comedy break from the woman in the middle." It was like this every time. They thought my presentation was funny and adorable. I would laugh and say, "Thank you."

When you don't know the language, you need a higher level of awareness to recognize what makes other people happy or angry. Being alert to the little details makes you feel that you're present and trying your best. You have to see how they think and then make yourself compatible with them. My Turkish friends tell me all the time. "You are so *uyumlu.*" Compatible.

Many Syrians here are struggling with coexistence. People are always telling my family and me, "Turkish people are not friendly. How have you made so many friends among them?" I relate it to a verse in the Quran. God took a bad thing from the Prophet Muhammad's chest. The angels cleaned it and returned it back to him. I believe that this means giving something from yourself and taking something from others. You're cleaning that thing with this community, taking it from them, and then putting it inside yourself.

If you don't open yourself up, you're not going to live happily here. If you don't share your palette, you'll remain the same painting. Mix your colors with them. Don't stay one color. Sometimes you need a bit of varnish, a bit of oil, maybe a bit of water. You have to take on some new mediums and give up some mediums. If you have your palette ready, then you can put yourself out there. You can be drawn with. You can be colored on. You can be added to. Our intuition is to try to control things, but you just have to trust the process. Some watercolors dry ugly and some dry beautiful. The important thing is that you did what you could do.

Rima

BEIRUT, LEBANON

L iving in Lebanon is a roller coaster. For me, Hezbollah is the main challenge. The other day I was in a shared taxi and overheard a guy saying on the phone, "I just got back from Syria, and my cousins are going there soon." They're all Hezbollah fighters. I thought, "I don't want to know this!" But the problem is that I actually *do* want to know this, and that is why I live in Lebanon.

Once, I was in Dahiyah* and I was walking and saw a poster. It was a photo of a seventeen-year-old guy. The picture was under the Assad regime's flag. It said "Hezbollah, Martyrs of Sayda Zeinab." The seventeen-year-old was barely smiling. I stopped and stared at his eyes because I wanted to make some sort of connection. The poster was next to this door, which seemed to be his house. It was a narrow street in this poor neighborhood, with writing all over the walls.

I looked at the door and then looked at the picture. And then looked at the door again and looked at the picture again. I tried to imagine him living there. I thought about the people he killed before he himself got killed. I wanted him to say anything to make me forgive. I thought, "You're too young to die. Do you even know why you went to Syria to fight?"

---

* Dahiyah is the majority-Shi'i southern suburb of Beirut, where many are supporters of Hezbollah and the movement has a strong presence.

The first time I went to Dahiyah, I didn't want to be friendly. I didn't want to see their human side. Now, every time something bad happens in Syria and I want to escape, I call someone to go to Dahiyah with me. It makes me feel less angry at the world. I try to dig deep, find common ground, feel calm. Maybe I feel as bad for them as I do for myself. I ask people for directions because they're very friendly. Sometimes I even ask for directions when I know where I'm going, just to have friendly human contact. And I ask myself: "Did this person go and fight in Syria? Do they believe in that fight?"

If you ask people from Dahiyah, they'll say that they're trying to protect their land from terrorists: "We're fighting them in Syria before they can come here." A taxi driver once told me that a group of one hundred people were coming from Syria to kill Lebanese in Dahiyah. This is like science fiction, but I try to understand why they believe it. I try to understand that they're victims too.

I DON'T want to forgive. But I do want to confront myself with these questions. Beirut is the place for that. Once, I was at a bar and was dancing and just wanted to forget. Then they started playing a song about Hezbollah having a great victory. What victory? Victory over what? I started throwing things and then just sat down and sobbed. I cried my heart out. People came toward me, and I yelled at them to leave me alone. It was such a surprise. You're at a bar and something takes you *right* there.

Sometimes, the surprise goes in the other direction. Once, I went to buy something. The man at the store was curious and started a conversation with me. It was a Shiʻi neighborhood, and I didn't think he'd be friendly. But I decided that I wasn't going to lie and I talked to him about what people are suffering in Syria. I was expecting a fight, but the guy said, "I respect you so much." He explained that his wife is from Syria, and he's standing with the people there.

This is Beirut. It's very different from any other city. It's always surprising you. You're never bored. No day is the same as another. Any interaction—in a taxi, in a grocery store—can change your whole day. The fact that a lot of Lebanese are racist toward Syrians is a given. I've collected a lot of experiences with racism over the years here. Now I feel like I can look at someone, make eye contact, and, in a fraction of a second, I can tell if the person is racist or not.

It's been good for me to come here and talk to people and be more connected to what they're thinking and feeling. It's been tough, but it made it easier to cope when we lost. I'm not in a bubble where everyone agrees. Here you get the full range. I couldn't imagine having lived anywhere besides Beirut these past years. In the end, losing was easier here.

IV

LOSING

ALHAKAM, AHMED, BASHAR, SHERRY, HANI, KOVAN, SARA M., ALI, LINA

In the context of Syrian displacement, losing home has myriad meanings. People forced to flee usually abandoned their physical houses and apartments and most or everything inside it. Some carried with them only what they could hastily fit in a suitcase. Others carried nothing because they were certain that they would return soon.

Many refugees' homes are not simply left behind but cease to exit altogether. According to the calculations of geographer Leïla Vignal, a quarter of Syria's pre-2011 urban housing was destroyed in the war.[1] While many homes were damaged by missiles and bombs, others suffered less obvious demises. Upon retaking control of opposition areas, regime forces typically looted deserted homes of everything from appliances to silverware to copper wire torn from their insides. They sometimes transferred razed plots to politically connected tycoons to redevelop for profit. Even when refugees' homes remained standing, they could become inaccessible. The Syrian government has issued dozens of decrees enabling it to confiscate land, including by imposing new procedures for registering property ownership that are impossible for displaced persons to complete. All of this points to an important corrective to rhetoric about returning refugees "back home": too often, refugees have no home to which to return.

Physical homes, of course, signify much more than wood and plaster. They can be the repository of a lifetime's work and care, encompassing the stories lived within their walls, a family's embeddedness in a neighborhood, and more. In the narratives that follow, Alhakam describes his unbreakable bond to the house that he, his father, and his siblings meticulously restored in the Aleppo Old City. Houses such as these, he tells us, are made homes by the pride invested in them and the memories uniquely attached to them. From Jordan, Ahmed and Bashar discuss how losing home shoulders them with a need to preserve those memories, even when it might bring them greater solace to forget. In Lebanon, Sherry describes a special event that recreates a Syrian home under harrowing bombardment. She sees how even memories of war elicit emotions that connect people to their past homes and to each other.

Like the weight of memory, losing home can entail another unseen burden: guilt. From Chicago, Hani expresses how many Syrians wonder why they survived while others did not; why they got out while others got stuck; why they met with the means to build new lives while others are trapped in conditions that hold them back. Feelings of doubt, remorse, and culpability—even when not grounded in any wrongdoing—point to an often-hidden aspect of losing. As consequential as people's feelings of loss can be the sense that they did not lose as much as others did.

As Hani explains, losing home is about losing people: those left behind, those who moved elsewhere, and those who did not make it. Losing home can carry a distinctly political meaning, as well. This comes to the fore among Syrians who found a new kind of home in the emancipatory experience of revolution, only to be deprived of that home too. Having made it from his imprisonment in Greece to residency in Sweden, Kovan grapples with what it means to lose hope and home at the same time. Sara M., separated and then reunited with Abu Tarek, similarly wonders what being removed from Syria means for her as a person devoted to working for Syria's freedom.

Losing a home means losing part of oneself, which can raise difficult questions about the degree to which one could be one's true self in that home in the first place. From India, Ali recalls Syria as a place where he was not accepted and from which he could not wait to escape. He misses it, nonetheless. In Germany, Lina feels that she is no longer the person she was in Syria. With time and distance, however, she stitches together fragments of her past and present into a new identity.

Moving forward in the work of making home involves mourning for what cannot be brought along or perhaps no longer remains. Stories about losing home brim with a heavy sadness. Yet they are also stories of discovery. The loss of what once was can impel one to look for hints of the familiar in foreign spaces or to find novel possibility in the unfamiliar. And it can lead one to make peace with loss itself, to accept that certain elements of home cannot be retrieved, and to uncover those aspects that can be reimagined and built anew.

Alhakam

My family's home is in Old Aleppo. One by one, we were all forced to leave it. Later, barrel bombs ate away at the house. The earthquake in 2023 completed the job, bringing down the roof of what used to be my bedroom.

Still, I remain attached. It's like an umbilical cord keeps me connected to Aleppo. Sometimes it feels like I never left. I still see it in my dreams a lot. Like a lot, a lot. Maybe once a week, I have a dream where I see myself in our house.

Our house in Aleppo, that very house, is still very much home for me. I painted so many rooms. I changed the glass of so many windows. I chiseled the frame for the sewers, the floor, the toilet. I mended the stones and filled the plaster between them.

It's been years since I left. Why don't I just give up? What are the chances of it ever becoming my home again? Why don't my sisters and brothers and I just sell it? I need to buy a home here in Europe, where I actually live. But here I'm just a passerby. I can't decorate any place because I know I won't be there long. Maybe if I get to the point where I own something here, I'll find peace with the idea of home. But I don't have that feeling yet. If I go back to Aleppo one day, I will find it to be no less a home than it was before. And I will still be very much tied to that place.

Ahmed

ZARQA, JORDAN

You can take anything with you when you cross the border, except your sense of homeland. The homeland becomes a memory. Imagine carrying all those memories on your shoulders. Memories of your house, of everyone you knew, of everything that ever crossed your path. You carry it all, and it becomes exhausting.

That's what it means to leave your country under circumstances like we did. Maybe it's different if you move to some place where you can live a normal life. Where you become a citizen and have rights, and so on. But here our lives are difficult. We're always making comparisons. "If I were in my own country—in my home—my needs might be met." That's not the case here.

When you're in a situation like ours, you try as hard as you can to forget the homeland, but you can't. The homeland is a companion that you can't let go. It's painful, but you nurture that pain. And the more exhausting the pain becomes, the more you nurture it. You torture yourself. It's masochism. That's the best way to describe our sense of homeland. It's masochism, but there's a reason behind the masochism: being without a homeland is terrifying. You need the pain of your memory of the homeland because it's even more painful to be without any homeland at all. Pain is better than nothingness.

Bashar

JORDAN

When you get hungry, you eat to satisfy your hunger. But how do you satisfy loss of appetite? That's the first phase of being a refugee: pain to the point of losing your passion for life. In the second phase, the feeling of *ghurba** fades a little. But still, you're a stranger. You always remain a stranger.

To me, my homeland is my house in Syria. After we left, they wrecked our house. Some of our relatives sent us photos. The whole area was bombed. A tank broke our lemon tree and our olive trees died. Everything was stolen. Our clothes, our furniture. Even the house's serenity was stolen. Sometimes a place can long for the souls of the people who lived there, just like those people long for their place.

I was thirteen years old when the war broke out. In 2012, my father was arrested. Until today, we have no news about him. That was one of the reasons we left Syria. It was no longer safe for my family. My mother decided that we should leave, but she was hesitant. She said, "How can we leave your father in Syria? But how can I leave you here under fire?" Leaving was a difficult decision, but it was the right one. We didn't know whether my father was alive or dead. She said to my

---

* The Arabic word *ghurba* means "alienation," "homesickness," or "separation." Coming from the same etymological root as "strange," it implies a state of estrangement or of being a stranger or foreigner in a land far from home.

siblings and me, "You are present. You are alive. For your sake, it's best that we leave."

In Jordan, we went to the Zaatari Camp* and then moved out to a city. We moved between many different houses until we finally found a house where we lived for six years. The whole neighborhood was Syrian. When we had to leave that house, we cried. It felt like it did when we left our house in Syria. I get very attached to places when I form memories there. But all those emotions are branches from the original tree: my house in Syria, and the people I loved there.

That's a refugee's life. Always moving. Always on the go. No stability. A refugee gets attached to a place, but then has to leave and feels like a stranger all over again. Refugees are always trying to migrate somewhere they can settle down—not because they want to terminate their longing but because they cannot. Wherever I go, the memory of Syria stays within me. Syria's olive oil tastes different. Its vegetables taste different. One of my Syrian classmates here in Jordan once told the teacher, "The sun in Syria is prettier."

After the war began in Syria, schools shut down. I was out of school for two years. When we got to Jordan, I did tenth and eleventh grade, but my family was in a tough economic situation, so I had to quit. Later, I went back and finished high school, but universities here are really expensive and there are very few scholarships. I kept applying and getting rejected. I'd email universities in Europe and write, "I'm a refugee. I want to resume my education. Help me." I never got any response. I kept applying for scholarships in Jordan. Finally, I got one.

Jordan is a good country. But not everyone I love is here. Our neigh-

---

* In 2012, Jordan opened the Zaatari refugee camp about 7.5 miles from the Syrian border. The camp's population grew to some 200,000 people before stabilizing to 80,000, with tents gradually replaced with metal caravans. In 2014, Jordan established a second camp in the desert near the town of Azraq, and it also grew to house about 45,000 Syrian refugees. Many Syrians who entered Jordan irregularly were transported to the Zaatari or Azraq camps for processing. They were permitted to relocate outside the camp under certain conditions, including having a legal sponsor.

bors are not here. I can't bring my house from Syria here or the olive trees or the flowers from our garden. I can't bring my sister who fled to Lebanon and whose kids I only know through video calls. And my father remains in Syria. Anywhere I live will feel temporary until we are all able to meet again, which is basically impossible. So even if I settle somewhere, something will always be missing. That's how a refugee feels: something is always missing. The only solution to the void is to lose your memory.

Sherry

BEIRUT, LEBANON

During the final assault on Ghouta,* there was an odd, respectful silence in Beirut. Even in taxis, people were quiet. When the bombing became very intense, people from Ghouta were saying that bombs dropped every seven minutes. There were seven minutes between explosions. I felt like we needed to do something. We planned an event called "Seven Minutes."

I tried to recreate something like the basement shelters where people were living in Ghouta. We had the exhibit in the basement of a theatre. Curtains separated the space into rooms. We had some very basic bread, made with the kind of flour that they were using under siege. There was a mattress in the corner. We had speakers that played the sound of shelling. It started faint and then got louder and louder and louder.

We told visitors to come in, move around, explore freely. People in Ghouta were talking about how terrible the smell was in the basements. I tried to recreate the smell. I have three cats and collected their dirty

---

* Rebels pushed Assad regime forces from Eastern Ghouta, a region ringing the outskirts of Damascus, in late 2012 and early 2013. Thereafter, the regime put the area under sustained siege, including attacking it with chemical weapons in August 2013. In February 2018, the regime launched a major offensive and heavy bombing campaign to recapture the area. It succeeded that April in what was considered one of the regime's most significant and brutal victories in the war.

litter for ten days, leaving it on my balcony. I brought that to the base-ment. Once when we were setting up, one of the guys was going to leave the basement to go to the bathroom. I told him, "No, pee here."

People came to the site. They were very, very respectful, but also distant. Most barely moved. When the sound of shelling reached the peak, many people practically froze in one spot. But I remember that one woman walked directly to the side of the room and sat down. There were shadows and light. And in that moment, I saw this dark ghost of her. She curled up in a ball, hugged her knees, and started to sob. She was crying and shaking, shaking and crying. She hadn't been through shelling before, but you could tell that she was trying to go there in her mind.

The event started conversations. The guy who worked at the theatre came to me and said, "I listen to these things on the news, but this took me back to my childhood during the Lebanese civil war. You're going through what we went through. But we forget what it feels like when it's not happening to us here and now."

So many Syrians came to the event. People even came in groups from the Bekaa Valley, on the other side of Lebanon. Some said that they wanted to come because it felt like the closest thing to home. Some felt like it was a way of saying goodbye because they don't think they'll go back again.

Hani

CHICAGO, USA

When you're inside the conflict or you're escaping, you think only of survival. It's fight or flight. Your system protects you and shuts down completely. Your brain says, "Throw this to the back of your mind. Don't think about it now." You don't think about what is happening or who is left behind.

Then, when you've settled somewhere, it comes back to you. You start remembering the details. So many details. It comes back in different ways. Sometimes it comes back heavily. Sometimes slowly.

I think guilt is part of life for everybody who survived, even if they don't recognize it yet. We'll always feel like, "I could have done something differently" or "That guy was arrested because of me." You think, "I could have helped this one person, but didn't." Then you try to trace that person again and you can't find him.

There will always be some formula in my head in which I'm the reason that somebody didn't make it. Like, that commander, Abu Jaber. He was always doing crazy stuff, like going to some regime checkpoint where there was no way he could get out alive. When I was there, I stopped him from those shenanigans. When I left, he went out and did something like that. He went to a checkpoint in the open desert, where you can see who's coming from ten miles away. And that one killed him. If I'd been there, I would have said, "C'mon man, this is stupid. Don't do it."

That's how we die. People died and that death didn't lead to any result. I feel bad. I just feel bad for them and their families. I think, "You didn't have to die. You could have left with me and survived." I carry that with me every day. I think we all do. I don't know how we live day-to-day, but we do.

I feel guilty for the people who died, for the people left behind, for the people who've been in camps for ten years. I think everyone should feel guilty for people who are now in situations without hope. There is guilt for the general loss. We didn't win a single battle. We lost the media battle, the economic battle, the political battle, the military battle. We lost our country, our cities, our homes, our friends. Some people feel like they lost themselves. Especially the older generation, like my dad. He loved his place, his community, his land. Now he doesn't feel like himself anymore. There is a lot of guilt for that, as well.

Guilt lives with me. And guilt makes you doubt things, doubt yourself. You wonder, "Why did we do any of this?" We lost so much and for nothing. The whole conflict started for a reason, and we came out empty-handed.

This is what they don't understand in the countries where Syrians are now living. They think that, when you arrive somewhere, you should just switch your mode completely. Speak German within six months, become very open, talk to people. But people left an entire life behind them. Most host countries don't want to hear this. They're like, "You're safe now. Why are you being so negative? You should be happy." Yes, of course I should be happy. I am happy. But I'm also guilty and sad. All of this challenges you. It challenges your religion, your beliefs, everything. Some people survive that challenge and succeed. Some do not.

Kovan

BORLÄNGE, SWEDEN

I went to Sweden because that's where my brother and sister were. I started working with the same journalism organization I'd worked with in Syria. After I got my Swedish residency permit, I went back to Turkey. Our organization started training journalists, and one of our achievements was to include citizen journalists too. But I started to lose hope. The political situation, Obama, chemical weapons, the world . . .* Our friends died, but nothing changed. Even the organizations that we worked with started to become bureaucratic and corrupt.

I'd had dreams that we'd return to Syria one day, but the dreams slipped further away. I decided to go back to Sweden. It wasn't clear to me then, but I was becoming depressed. In Sweden, I started studying the language. I worked at McDonald's for six months. I still wanted

---

* In August 2013, the Syrian Army launched a chemical weapons attack on rebel-controlled areas in the suburbs of Damascus, killing more than 1,400 people, including 400 children. US President Barack Obama's prior declarations that use of chemical weapons in Syria was a "red line" raised expectations that the United States would respond with military strikes. After two weeks of debate and diplomacy, the Obama administration announced that it had instead reached an agreement with Russia to destroy Syria's chemical weapons stockpile. The decision not to intervene militarily against Assad deepened despair among many Syrian oppositionists, who believed that it communicated to the regime and its allies that they could kill with impunity.

to pursue my passion for computers, but I'd only finished three years of engineering school before the revolution began. Sweden didn't recognize my university credits. I had to start over from senior year of high school. I eventually restarted university, but my mood kept going down. The other students were eighteen. I was almost twenty-eight and the only one speaking broken Swedish. After so many years had passed, my passion for computers was gone.

By the second semester I was feeling down. Really, really, really down. Depression brings one problem after another, like dominoes. I quit the university. I started drinking and using drugs. I struggled to pay rent. For six months, all my mail was bills. I couldn't open anything. Depression changes your personality. I started having problems with my family. My ability to speak with people was ruined. I met other Syrians living in Europe and realized that most were dealing with the same thing. Everyone was depressed. We were like animals ripped out of their natural habitat. If you take a polar bear and put it in Africa, it'll die after a few days because it can't acclimate to its new environment.

In Syria, I never lived a day alone. I'd go to the store and say hi to everyone. Here, I became alone with my thoughts for the first time. I'd just think and think and think. It was actually worse when I went to parties. I'd be hanging out and drinking with all of these people from different nationalities and look around at their happiness. I didn't understand why I couldn't feel the same way.

I used to have big hopes and dreams, but I've given up on them. For years I was ready to do anything for the revolution. The revolution was so beautiful. We felt that we were changing something not just in Syria but also within ourselves. We came out of our shells. People discovered that they were photographers or journalists or filmmakers. We started to get to know each other as Syrians. Before, there was a barrier, something that prevented us from speaking to others. As a Kurd, I knew Kurdish people in my circle, but didn't mix much with others.*

---

* The Kurdish ethnic group is a minority population in Turkey, Iraq, Iran, and Syria. In Syria before 2011, approximately 8–10 percent of the country's population was Kurdish, some 300,000 of whom were stateless stemming from

During the revolution, I would go to the homes of Druze or Christians. I met amazing people whom I never even knew existed.

☺

WHEN I look back, I ask, "What was it all for?" I think that Syrians who are not honest with themselves are going to remain in this cycle forever. I've seen a lot of people who are living in the past. I was one of them. I'm better now. I have a kind of stability in Sweden. Maybe it's not stability as much as acceptance of reality. I started being realistic, telling myself, "That's enough, stop chasing fantasies." I've become content with not dreaming.

I'm secure, but not at ease. In Syria, I used to explore trees, touch them, look at their details. There isn't an area in Syria where I haven't held its rocks and learned about their details. Here, I don't interact much with nature. There are so many trees, but I never touch them. I've visited many cities in Sweden, but I've never paid any attention to their rocks. They stir no reaction in me.

I'm attached to the past. I love the home that I used to have in Syria. But now? If I went back, I wouldn't play with the trees or rocks. I don't even know anyone in Qamishli now. I used to know every detail of the area and now I know nothing. Everyone was forced out. I'd feel like a complete stranger. It can never be home again. Never. To be honest, I would never even go back because I don't want to experience that feeling. It's not even a matter of Syria being safe or not. I wouldn't return because of the pain it would cause.

---

a 1962 government decision to strip the citizenship of some Kurds. While many Kurdish individuals joined the uprising, key Kurdish political parties steered a course between regime and opposition in an effort to advance Kurdish national claims to autonomy in the regions where the Kurdish population is concentrated.

Sara M.

GAZIANTEP, TURKEY

After I made it across the border to Turkey, I stayed with a Syrian family. For the first two days, I just slept and kept taking showers. I kept wearing the hijab that I'd worn while escaping from Syria. After three days, I asked the mother in the family, "Is there a hair stylist around here?" I got my hair done and started to feel like myself again.

Then I got back to work. I got a registration permit and licensed the organization that Abu Tarek and I worked with in Syria. I started communicating with people inside Syria to provide services to people there.

But I felt so lonely. I didn't know anyone. In Turkey, you become just one number among so many numbers. In my country before the revolution, I was Rasha. I was living in my own community. In the revolution, people got to know Sara and they also became my own people. We were working on the ground to make a change and felt strong. But that was inside Syria. Inside *that* geography. It's totally different to be looking in from the outside. Here we became powerless and vulnerable.

SOME OF the guys in our group in Syria got detained. It became impossible for Abu Tarek to stay any longer. For three months, he kept trying to travel to Lebanon, but couldn't make it out. Then he decided to travel to Turkey. When he arrived, I felt like a part of me came back. We became Siamese twins again.

Now we're trying to start a movement here. And if we can, in other diaspora countries where Syrians are located too. But it's difficult. We no longer see ourselves in the revolution. We changed from people who were working in the revolution to people who are working to support the revolution from afar.

The most important thing at this stage is to protect the last bit of hope that people have left. All we can do is live on hope.

Ali

Home is a weird thing. It combines the things I love most with the things that hurt me the most. It's funny how I miss the place I spent my whole life trying to escape. That is the paradox. Home is a kind of safety, even though you hate it and you know you're not safe. Home is the people who know you, even though they didn't know me completely.

I was very shy. I was interested in books and coloring. I grew up with Britney Spears, Shakira, Enrique Iglesias, and sitcoms like *Friends*. I'd hang out almost entirely with girls. Later, I struggled with my sexuality. It made me so afraid. Growing up in a small, remote village, you think you're the only person on the entire planet like this. You think, "Is my entire existence wrong? Did God make a mistake?" In TV shows, the gay character is always portrayed as effeminate or sissy. That's the only way to be gay. And a gay person is definitely going to hell. You see this and, obviously, you hate yourself.

When I was eighteen, my mom came up to me and said, "You know I love you and I accept you. I want to ask you something." I knew where she was going. She said, "Are you gay?" To this day, I still remember the word that she used. In the Arab world, you call a queer or gay person *"shath."* Literally, it means irregular or abnormal. She didn't use that word. She said *"mithli,"* which means homosexual. It was amazing that she used that word. I didn't answer, exactly. I just hugged her and cried.

I WENT to college in the city. I wouldn't say that I was bullied, but I'd get looks. People would leave their bags in the auditorium. Twice I came back for my bag and found notes saying, "Go to hell" or something like that. I was like, "Why?" Who would do this? Where do they get the energy to do this? People say that the opposite of love is not hate but indifference. Hate requires energy.

For the first year and a half of college, I lived at home. Then I met my first boyfriend. Gradually, I stayed every fourth night at his place. Then I moved in. He made me accept myself. He made me accept that we deserve to love and to be loved. My parents loved him and would come over sometimes. When I think about happy times, these are some of the few that come to mind. My mom would come cook and the three of us would sit together. The people who mattered most to me existed at that time in that one room. There was something very beautiful about that. That's my idea of home.

I'M NOT going to lie; I also associate home with pain. In Syria, I spent my whole life trying to leave. When I was sixteen, I thought, "Gay people only exist in Europe and the US. I need to get out." Then in my twenties, I thought, "Life here is economically and socially unbearable. I need to get out." It wasn't just because of the war. My mom and dad didn't have a happy marriage. Our home was dysfunctional.

Hope is very dangerous. If you don't hope, you'll never be disappointed. When I got the scholarship to study in India, I was full of excitement. I thought that all of this would be behind me and I'd have a new place and a new life. That didn't happen. Coming from Syria, my standards for quality of life were not that high. But I remember when we arrived in India and they were driving us from the airport, and I saw people who were abjectly poor. They were washing clothes in puddles of rainwater. I felt my heart fall, physically. I was silent. At the hostel, the rooms were very dusty, and the mattresses didn't have bedsheets.

I just started bawling. I bawled and bawled for days. I'd made it out of Syria only to get to another place that wasn't much better. I felt the finality of it all, like the cord with my parents had been cut. I felt born again, like I was in a womb and then was out of it. I was on my own. I had to make my own decisions. I was not home anymore but the hope of making a new home shattered.

There were about twenty-five Syrian students. Then another group came, with more than one hundred Syrian students. It felt like a mini-Syria. I couldn't be myself. I couldn't behave the way I wanted to. I had to watch my tone and how I walked and talked. I felt that whole thing, all over again.

⊙

I'M IN a better place now. Last year I applied again to many scholarships. I had to be careful with what I applied for, because the application fees are a lot for me. I got a partial scholarship to do a diploma in liberal studies and moved to a new university. This new campus is very nice and open-minded. There are some people with whom I can be myself. There are moments when I feel content.

I made the choice to come here and I don't regret it. But the program ends this summer. I don't know what I'll do after that. I'm like a deer in headlights. I live in constant, paralyzing fear. I just don't want to have to go back to Syria. No matter how much I miss it. I feel almost as trapped now as I felt back home. For, me, "trapped" is a synonym for Syria. It reminds me of this line from a TV series that is very close to my heart: "To live is to survive unfair choices." I think a lot of people in Syria can relate to that. I hated that I was born there. I hated that we were poor. I hated that there was war.

During the years that I've been away, I've thought about home many times. And when I think about it, I see only the good parts. It's funny how we tend to romanticize home. What I miss are not things, but situations. I miss sitting with my grandmother and having tea together on her balcony. I used to study on that balcony, walking back and forth the length of it. I would look up at the beautiful view. I can tell you every inch of it. There's a hill and then a valley and then the opposite hill. There's the street and the houses. I remember the transition to sunset: How the sun would drag and turn into twilight. The sound of children finishing whatever they were playing. The mothers calling them home. I love the colors. There are so many trees, and each tree has its own shade of green. In autumn, olive trees remain green and some other trees turn red and yellow. I can describe the feeling of home as those warm, autumn colors. Yellow, orange, gold.

My mother says that her only wish is to see me before she dies. At the same time, she tells me, "Please, find a way to never come back." She knows that I can never be happy there. Life there is not life. I don't know what it is, but it's not life. My family in Syria is alive only because they're not dead. I would do anything to see my mom and grandmother again. But I don't want to go back.

Lina

BERLIN, GERMANY

I'd be lying if I said that I'm Lina. Here in Germany, I'm not the Lina I was before I left Syria. There are a lot of pages of Lina that I can't open in Germany because it's too painful. To continue, sometimes you can't keep being yourself. There are aspects of my personality that I need to forget or kill to create a new Lina who can live here.

In Syria, I considered myself a strong person. Someone who rebelled against social norms. I lived in a conservative area. I was the first girl to ride a bike on the street, and then a lot of women rode bikes after I did. I dyed my hair yellow and changed my appearance every day. I fell in love with a person from a different religion, and we fought our families to get married. I viewed all of these things as accomplishments for that time and that society.

When I first arrived in Germany, I was always crying, crying, crying. I had zero self-confidence and couldn't take a step forward. Why was this happening to me here when it never happened in Syria? I'd complete my application to start university again and then be too afraid to submit it. I just wanted my mom. In Syria, I didn't answer to anyone. Here, I couldn't even pick out my own clothes. I'd video-call my mom or sister, "What do you think, is this nice or not?" I couldn't drink a cup of coffee without someone to talk to. I'd call my family, but they didn't have the time. After all, they're in Syria! "What's wrong with her? Why is she calling every minute?" I'd get sad. "Why aren't they sympathizing with me? They've forgotten me!"

157

I couldn't make decisions. My husband would ask me, "What do you want for dinner?" I don't know. I don't know what I want. I don't even know why I'm here. Why am I walking down the street alone? I completely lost my identity. Maybe it was because, in Syria, my family was standing behind me. Even if I was fighting with them, at the end of the day there was always a home I could go back to.

◎

MY HUSBAND came to Germany first, and then I came on a visa. That meant that I was allowed to return to Syria. At first, I went back and forth each year. My trips were for healing, recuperating. I'd fill up on Syria so I could take it back with me. But when the time came to say goodbye, I'd relive the pain all over again. It felt like reopening a wound that had just started to heal.

While I kept pulling myself toward Syria, my husband was pulling himself away. That was the struggle inside our house. He wanted to forget. For him, phone calls to his family in Syria were a form of trauma. So, I became a form of trauma to him too. Eventually, I felt that if I kept going to Syria every year, I'd stay stuck in the same cycle. I'd keep reliving everything and never find myself. I didn't want to see my family and then have to leave them again.

It's been three years since the last time I returned. It was hard, like killing someone. But that time has rebalanced me. I needed that disconnect to be able to see clearly. I was able to see Syria from a distance and saw that I was living a lie in believing I was happy there. I thought that I was a strong woman, but if I ever encountered a problem, I would have no rights.

◎

IN SYRIA, I knew how to work within existing institutions, despite their oppressiveness. Here, everything is better for you as a person in every way. But I don't know how to maneuver. You have to learn everything from scratch.

In Syria, I was studying art. I wasn't achieving anything in particular, but just sitting with my family was worth the world. Life in Germany is a schedule. It's like someone is standing over you with a stick. I'm always thinking, "Lina, before the month ends, you need to finish X, Y, Z." This isn't life. It's a list that you think about night and day.

When you're in *ghurba*, you need to achieve something. If you're not achieving something, then you might as well go back to your homeland and be with your family. I'm always battling with myself, seeing something I lack. Maybe I should work on my German. Maybe I need to learn English. I tell myself that I'm living countless blessings that others don't have: electricity, water, opportunities for work. I try to think about it rationally: "Lina, you should be happy because you're not in Syria." You're forced to build a fake person with fake happiness in this place. As a Syrian in Germany, even happiness is an obligation.

Sometimes, I struggle with Syrians here more than with Germans or foreigners. We aren't very accepting sometimes, even of each other. We don't know how to work together because we don't have the culture of free organizations or free expression. We're coming from a dictatorship, so everyone wants to be the leader. Or you just follow along, lying to yourself so you get by.

After I came to Germany, I started to meet other Syrians. I thought, "We don't have people like this or that in Syria! It's impossible that they come from the same country that I do." We all thought that we were unified, and then the war started and we realized that we aren't similar at all. They have their struggles, and you have your struggles. They have their mental illnesses, and you have yours. They are in one bubble, and you are in another. You slowly find yourself estranged, pushed into your own corner. When you meet Syrians in Germany, you try to search for who you were in Syria. But you can't find it.

Relationships are stronger when they have spontaneity and you're not keeping tabs. Those relationships are hard to come by. I miss someone saying, "Hey Lina, I'm coming over just because I want to hang out with you." And when I say that I'm not free, they come over anyway.

I follow online groups for Syrian women in Germany. You won't believe the number of posts like: "Ladies, please, I just need a friend to walk with." You find that a lot. "I decided to take this step and reach out to you all because I want a friend." They are women from all backgrounds, and they just don't want to be alone. And then when they find people who are like them, they close the circle. There are times when I walk in the park and see a group sitting together. I want to ask, "Is it okay for me to sit with you?" I've never asked because it would look strange. But I see them happy, and I have that feeling: "Could I just sit with you for a little?"

I don't miss the air of the streets in Syria like I did the first year or two here. I miss my family. I miss hearing stories about this or that person. I miss being able to knock on my aunt's door unannounced and rest on the sofa. After I came to Germany, I realized that I had been spoiled and never knew it.

☉

WHEN SYRIANS get German citizenship they say, "I'm proud that I've become German." If I get citizenship, I don't think I'll be saying that. I'm not proud to be Syrian either. When I first came, I used to say, "I'm Syrian!" I was raised to believe that this was a great thing. Now that has been broken for me. Syria as a place and nation no longer adds anything to who I am. If you take me to Syria, I'm going to be happy with the people I miss. But I'll be rejecting the rules and everything related to them. What is belonging if you're fighting your society twenty-four hours a day?

I've evolved because of what I've been through. My mentality has changed. I've become half and half. I no longer belong here or there. My belonging is to myself. To the beliefs that I've built as a result of my experiences. A big part of identity is memory. How I was raised. How I developed my thoughts and beliefs. How I made friends. You need to come to terms with your memories so that you can build an identity at peace with a new society.

A lot of Syrians here erased their past. You ask someone his name and he says, "David." You say hello in Arabic, and he responds in German or English. He's trying to build a new life in a new society. He thinks that everything he endured brought him to this difficult point, so he hates everything. Even his name.

For a while, my husband didn't want to talk to his family in Syria. The way he was raised was eating at him. I stayed after him. It's better to come to terms with it. This is the new you. Tie it to the past in a healthy way, the best you can. You come from that society. Your mom and dad raised you that way because that's how they were raised. They didn't want to hurt you. They did what they thought was right.

I don't think your identity will be at peace if you erase your history. Deep down, that past is there. As much as you try to hide it, it's going to come up. Maybe in your dreams. Try to find yourself between here and there. Then you can enrich your identity instead of tearing it apart.

☙

WHEN WE first started learning German, they told us, "You need to speak German at home. You're never going to advance as long as you go home and speak to your partner in Arabic." I tried. I tried. But it didn't work at all. We'd speak two sentences and switch back to Arabic. I felt guilty for speaking my language, but I needed to be human.

In Syria, my family drinks maté.* I never used to drink it. Here, I started drinking it every morning and evening. Anytime my husband and I feel like we're suffocating, he says, "Do you want to drink maté?" I

---

* Maté, a tea-like beverage traditional in South America, is brewed from the dried leaves of the yerba maté plant. Many late nineteenth- and early-twentieth century migrants from Ottoman Syria and Lebanon to South America took up the drink and brought it back to their home countries, where it remains popular until today.

say yes, and I immediately feel like there are good things in life. I drink it and it brings me back to memories of my homeland and of people being together.

For New Years, I put up a tree like my mom used to do at home. During Ramadan, sometimes I have dinner at the right time to break the fast, even though we're not fasting. I'm not religious and my husband isn't even Muslim. But I try to put myself in the same context that my family is living in Syria, just to feel close to them.

There are television shows that I never used to watch in Syria, but I watch here. I talk to my mom and she says, "No, I didn't see that one." In Syria, I was like her. I was too busy with life to care about TV. But here I watch those programs a lot. You start to care about things you didn't care about back home. They tie you to it, remind you of it. It was part of what created a warm environment there, but you didn't notice it at the time. You try to bring it to your life now.

V

BUILDING

MEDEA, AHLAM, MAJDY,

SALMA, MARIAM, FATIMA, GHANI,

ALAA, HOUDA, NOUR, RIFAIE

"Building home" might elicit images of the brick, wood, and concrete of a physical dwelling. But it also signifies something more: the intimate and intangible process of building one's own self. A first home is typically the foundational environment in which children construct their personality and primary relationships. Leaving that home is a rite of passage for many young people as they set off to build themselves as independent adults. Getting one's own apartment for the first time, moving in with a partner, or moving away from a partner are all milestones of personal growth embodied in shifts in homeplaces. Even in the most stable of political settings, therefore, changing from one home to another can be a cause, effect, or marker of important personal change.

The connection between home-building and self-building is especially pronounced in contexts of forced migration. Refugees are violently, and sometimes suddenly, cut out of the encompassing worlds that had grounded their identities. They are thrust into foreign spaces where they are expected to conform to different ways of thinking and being. They might find that some elements of their former selves are impossible to recuperate in this new environment or perhaps are better left behind. However individuals respond to the personal dislocations wrought by physical dislocation, they are unlikely to emerge as exact replicas of who they were before.

Some of the raw material used in this self-building is cultural. Settling in a new country can bring one into contact with new assumptions, habits, behaviors, norms, and mentalities. All of this can challenge one's preexisting ideas about topics from religion to family relationships, gender roles, and the meaning of a good life. Alternatively, such new immersion might redouble people's commitment to the customs and beliefs that they bring from elsewhere—but now with a perspective that bears the imprint of having been tested in new ways.

The factors shaping personal change in refuge are also social and relational. For forced migrants separated from relatives and friends, exile can dare them to make home far from those who had always defined it. Experiencing such a transformation cannot but change people as individuals, as well. They might extract new strength from pushing forward alone or find love and support in surrogate families. To the degree that humans become who they are in interaction with others, the ways that displacement transforms communities and social bonds will affect how individuals build who they are in the world.

Yet another aspect of the simultaneous building of home and self is professional. A job can be a source not only of income but also identity, pride, and social status. In new countries, refugees can face steep obstacles to continuing in their prior occupations due to language barriers, legal restrictions, discrimination, unretrievable diplomas, or a host of bureaucratic demands for retraining and recertification. Given these challenges, displacement is frequently an experience of downward socioeconomic mobility. When conditions are favorable, however, the potential for achievement is immense. For example, more than half the refugees who arrived in Germany in 2015 had, five years later, learned German, become employed, and were paying taxes. More than 10,000 were enrolled in universities.[1] A decade after Syrians began fleeing in 2011, Turkey had registered some 14,000 new Syrian-owned firms and 30,000 Syrian university students.[2] These numbers testify to refugees' capacity to build themselves, even when violently plunged—to invoke the expression that Syrians often use in this context—*taht as-sifr* or "below zero."

Refugees' experiences of personal building in displacement vary with their own characteristics, the material and social capital that they possess, and the kinds of trauma they carry, as well as opportunities in the countries in which they settle. Stage in life matters too. For older people who have already invested decades in establishing themselves, the task of starting over might be too daunting. Those who feel that they are still at the outset of their life journeys, by contrast, might be able to rally the enormous energy required to push forward or into theretofore-unseen directions. All of this shapes what people see as home—be it the now-lost place where they became who they were or the new launching pad from which they can become who they still hope to be.

The narratives that follow delve into how changing experiences of home affect people's building of themselves as individuals, and vice versa. Medea finds compatibility with Istanbul by mixing her colors with Turkish society, but still wonders: if she returned to her home-land, would it feel like home? Trips to internally displaced people's camps in rebel-controlled northwest Syria help her develop a theory of home as where you grow. Ahlam is one of those internally displaced people. She lives with ongoing bombardment, economic precarity, and other daily insecurities, but discovers her calling as a teacher and leader and commits herself to staying.

Others trace experiences from their arrival in a foreign place, describing how the processes of building home and building their own personal strength proceed in tandem. Crossing the border as a teenager alone, Majdy finds a dilapidated and empty apartment. As he musters the independence and resourcefulness to establish a new life, the apartment becomes the home he worked to make. Salma similarly learns to navigate Amman on her own at a young age. She cultivates a love for the city, not despite the difficulties that it poses, but because those difficulties fortify her personality and readiness for new challenges. For Mariam as well, finding home is intertwined with finding her voice. Exhausted with tiptoeing around the relatives who reluctantly give her shelter after her husband's death, she relocates to a center for widows in Lebanon and thrives in its empowering community.

Speakers bring other personal and professional experiences to the fore, as well. In Jordan, Fatima moves from sorting tissues and documenting injured Syrians to translation work. She meets a new set of colleagues who test her beliefs and encourage her to dream again. Ghani, having endured torture in prison, travels to Jordan and then resettles in the United Kingdom, where he relaunches his barbering career and claims a new future. In Germany, Alaa still cannot comprehend why he was released from prison in Syria while his six relatives were not. Yet he converts tragedy into determination as he commits himself to achieving the educational goals that his imprisoned father had imagined for him. In Sudan, Houda's new experiences reinvigorate her religious convictions. Meanwhile, Nour, long after she was chased at her university and fled Syria, comes to question what religion means to her. Finally, Rifaie's life in Australia builds in new ways when he becomes a father. Still, the sting of separation from his mother and sister in Turkey continues to define home for him.

These stories show how displacement can impel people to adapt, develop, recommit, or reorient, and why these developments in identity carry implications for one's understanding of home. As much as making home is about connecting to a place, it is also an undertaking in self-discovery and growth. There are no shortcuts in this deeply personal process. And that, too, is part of what makes finding home after refugee flight both struggle and achievement.

Medea

ISTANBUL, TURKEY

The organization that I work for does projects in northwest Syria, where most people are internally displaced from other regions in Syria. My boss asked if I'd like to go, and I said yes. I feel at home in Istanbul, but I had this doubt inside me: If I went back to Syria, would I feel at home again there?

Before we crossed from the Turkish side, we had to get permission from the Turkish government. That really disturbed me. I thought, "Why do I need someone else's permission to go to my own country?" Then we entered Syria. The first thing I saw was the employee who stamped our papers. He was speaking Arabic! Syrian Arabic! I looked at him and it's like my eyes were hearts. I thought, "I'm so thankful that I'm meeting you!" And he was like, "Let me do my job. Next in line."

We got to the camps. I tried so hard to belong there. I tried to merge—to wear clothing like theirs and wear my hijab in the same style. But they looked at me like a stranger. They said, "Where are you from?"

I said, "I'm from Syria. I'm just like you!" I surprised myself when I said that. Literally, "I'm just like you."

There was one man who looked at me and said, "You're not from here, are you?"

I said, "No, but I'm Syrian."

And he said, "But you're not living *in* Syria."

I asked how he could tell. He said, "Your eyes look relaxed."

◎

I'VE BEEN back five or six times since then. Every time the children see me, they say, "Here comes the guest from abroad!"

Most of the camps are in empty desert, disconnected from everything else. They're in the middle of nowhere because that's the only land that people could use. The camps are a palette of three sad colors: the gray and beige of tents and the yellow road. And in winter, there's red mud.

On the outside, the tents are all the same. But from the inside, you see each person's personality. Older people don't put effort into making their tents look like a home because they don't believe that they should be living there in the first place. They keep saying, "I'm just waiting for the day we return home." But there is a new generation that grew up in this place. They've never spent time inside four walls and a ceiling. They don't really know their family's former home. It's all distant now.

One time, I was with three young women. They were so excited for me to see their tents. I was like the prize of the day. "I want to show you my tent!" "No, I want to show you my tent!" I went inside. One was getting married the following week and she'd drawn her and her fiancé's initials on the wall of the tent with buttons and beads. She said, "I gave it my own touch so it wouldn't be ordinary. I made it feel like home. And now it's ours."

◎

LIFE IN the camps is always the same. Our organization runs centers and classes. We do activities to make the kids feel happy. Once, we started playing some songs so they would dance and have fun. When we were starting to pack up, this little girl ran and jumped onto the speaker, holding it with her hands and feet. She said, "Please, don't take it away! We don't have any other sounds here." She'd heard something new and her mind started to work. It was giving her new colors. They're children and their minds are craving development. But in such an environment they can't develop.

This strengthened my theory about home. Home is about growing into a bigger person. Home is finding what a place can give you that can help you grow. When people feel that they have no more opportunities to grow, they want to go back to what they grew with in the past. That's why a lot of the older people say, "I miss my home, I miss my things." They don't have a new goal or a "future me" they want to become, so they remain attached to their old homes.

The first time I went to Syria with our organization, I thought, "Okay, I'm home now, I should feel at home." But I asked myself if I could stay and I couldn't. And that's because there is no chance to grow there. In that harsh environment, only the brave ones succeed to grow. They have dreams and will do whatever they can to keep making themselves grow bigger. When I ask those people, "Do you feel that you belong here?" They say, "No, this area is like a prison. We're just working to try to escape and get somewhere better."

Ahlam

IDLIB, SYRIA

We were displaced several times, and the camp was our last resort. It was near the border with Turkey, far from the air strikes and fighting. In a way, it was safe. We set up a tent like everyone else. Tents were so close together that your neighbor heard you even when you whispered. When it snowed, water would freeze on the sides of the tent. But then spring and summer passed, and I made my tent better. I organized it and planted mint and flowers in front. My tent became a paradise.

My son had a friend who needed help studying for exams. He asked, "Is it okay if I bring him home?" I said, "Of course." Then he brought more friends. The tent was small, and the number of students coming for lessons increased. At first, there were only boys. Then parents asked me to teach their daughters too. Then we started having lessons for the mothers. It became known which tent belonged to me: the teacher.

Organizations started to come to the camp. They opened something called the Women's Empowerment and Protection Center. It taught things like sewing and self-management. I interviewed and got the job as center supervisor. When they told me my salary, I cried out of happiness. I hadn't received a salary in so long. I built my capabilities and became strong. When that initiative ended, I found work in other organizations.

Now my kids are grown and I have grandkids. My kids say, "Mom, you've worked enough. Why don't you just take it easy?" I say, "No. No way." I'm still standing on my own two feet, I'm still able to provide. When you have love in your heart, it gives you energy.

I miss my home. Sometimes when I try to sleep, I remember our garden, how I used to water the flowers and grape vines. I remember the streets. I remember my friends who died or whose children died. I remember my brother who died.

I have a passport from when we lived in Libya before the war. I could have left to another country. But I feel like people here need my help more. The idea of leaving entices all of us. When the air strikes intensified, my kids blamed me. They said, "It's your fault, you didn't let us leave." I said, "If you leave and the doctor leaves and the teacher leaves, who will be left for the people struggling here?"

Every now and then, my kids say, "Look at our friends who went to Germany or Canada. They're living well." That's true. But in the end, people long for their country. When someone shows you an act of kindness, you must return the favor. This country gave me a lot. I lived abroad for sixteen years. That was enough. Mahmoud Darwish has a poem where he says, "I am the land, and the land is you." My belonging is to the land. In the end, the homeland lives within me, and I live in it.

Majdy

BEKAA VALLEY, LEBANON

After Malek was killed, I started going to school for only one reason: to tell people to join the protests. Because of that, my dad started receiving threats. He decided that I should leave the country. I woke up and my mom said, "There's a car downstairs waiting to take you to Lebanon." On the border, the driver said, "We're dropping you off here."

It was the first time I'd ever traveled. I didn't know where I was or what I was supposed to do. I didn't know anyone, so I started asking people on the street, "What town is this? What should I do? Where should I sleep?" A Syrian guy told me, "Don't book a hotel, rent a house instead. You'll be safe and no one will bother you." I was a little scared. I was in a strange country and couldn't tell if he was friend or enemy. But I kept talking to people and found a house to rent.

It was a terrible house. It stank and was always flooding. Moving in was the scariest thing in my life. I'd never lived alone before. It was the first time that I had to think about what to eat, about finding water to drink or shower. I didn't know how to cook anything. For a while, I ate only what I could eat straight from the package. When I finally got a plate, knife, spoon, and fork—when I was able to fry an egg—the house transformed from a source of fear to a source of safety. It became the home I worked to make.

I arrived in that house a boy, and that is where I started to gain a sense of responsibility. When I entered that house, it was a country and

I was its president. It was me, my true personality, not something I was creating to please others.

I'd write on sticky notes and stick them on the wall. I'd write, "Today this happened to me," and I'd write the date and time. I felt that anyone living in a house without paper and pencil would disappear. Because, if that person died, no one would be able to read about their lives. I thought if someone entered the house, he'd know my life and thoughts. One day, someone would be able to say, "There was a person named Majdy, and this is what he believed."

I started to buy things incrementally. One month, I bought a mattress. The next, a pillow. The next, a heater. I couldn't afford more than that. I bought a notebook and started writing in it every day. There are things that people are embarrassed to tell other people, but I wasn't shy to tell the notebook. I'd write, "I'm hungry and can't afford to buy food. I need to figure out how to make money." Or "Today I met a girl, and she's really pretty." I had no one to talk to, so I talked to the paper. These words made me feel something. They made me want to live for tomorrow. I'd write those words and wake up ready for the day.

The notebook accepted my thoughts and didn't make fun of me or tell me to stop. I can compare the notebook to Malek, my martyred friend. I used to tell Malek everything that happened to me. After Malek was killed, I had this notebook. This notebook was like Malek: it listened and knew every detail of my life. Until today, the notebook is the most precious thing I own. It has lived through everything that I've lived, both good and bad.

Salma

AMMAN, JORDAN

My older sister was in Germany, so I also studied German. I reached a strong level and applied for a visa to go to Germany. It came back just two days later: rejected.

I was like, "Okay. Let's be reasonable." I'm not someone to cry or complain. I toughen myself up, on my own. I went online and searched: "Where can Syrians go without a visa?" Names popped up: Sudan, Lebanon, Malaysia, and a lot of other countries. And Jordan. I'd always heard about Amman through its alternative music scene. I thought, "Okay, Amman. That's good. What universities do they have?"

I found the German Jordanian University. They require you to go to Germany for your senior year. I could make it to Germany, after all. The university didn't offer a major in drama, so I decided that I would study translation instead. It relates somehow to the arts and can lead to a good job with a good income. I thought, "My Syrian nationality isn't strong enough to secure my future, but at least I can get a degree that is strong. And I will find a way to work in theatre too."

☺

My visa application was rejected on a Sunday or Monday. By Thursday, I was in Amman. It was really scary for my parents to send their youngest daughter somewhere they knew nothing about. My father was freaking out. He came with me to Jordan. We found an apartment and then the university. Then he left, and I was alone.

I was scared. I didn't know anyone or anything. The only thing I knew was the grocery store downstairs from my house. I spent my first week just walking around the neighborhood and discovering places, and then getting food from that grocery store and coming home to cook.

I started at the university but didn't like studying translation at all. I felt that I was wasting my time and was never going to be an actor. But I said to myself, "I made this decision. Now what am I going do about it?"

I started to build connections. I found an NGO that offered internship opportunities. At the university, I joined the drama club. I started doing special effects makeup. Last year, I acted in my first play. After that, I acted in a short film. I made a lot of friends in the theatre scene. Now I'm learning singing and contemporary dance. I also play ukulele. Being an actor, you must be skilled in many things because you never know what you might need to play a role. I'm training myself in all these aspects so I can be a great artist someday.

◎

Now, Amman is my home. I love its chaos. There's a lot of construction, a lot of noise. There are cats everywhere. Plants grow wherever they can. The sounds, the colors, the people—I feel it all hugging me. I love these details.

I love Amman because this is where I became the person I am. It's my home because I came here at age eighteen and did everything on my own. What I accomplished was not because my family knew someone or because my sister helped me. No, I did it all by myself. And I did it in a country that's not really safe. Especially for a young girl working in theatre, because sometimes you get home very late. I'm not scared anymore because I've made friends who are like family. If anything happens, I have people I can call immediately. But even without them, I know how to be tough in the streets.

That's why I call Amman home. Without being here, I would never have had the experiences that have shaped me. I wouldn't be as strong as I am today. Now I can live anywhere and do anything. Imagine what I can accomplish once I get to a country that provides me with safety and my rights?

Years ago, home was provided for me. But once I lived on my own, home changed. I miss my family, but when I go back to visit them, I don't feel at home. At the same time, I want to move forward. I want to learn more, know more. If I continue to live here, I'll be limited to the things that I already know. But wherever I go, this will always be my first home. Because this is where I began.

Mariam

The shelling started on our street. Everyone left in a different direction. Our family got separated. I don't know anything about what happened to my husband. I don't know if he's still alive or got killed. Peace be upon him.

I went to stay with my sister-in-law. I was six months pregnant with my daughter. After I gave birth, I couldn't get her milk or diapers. I had no money. What could I do?

My sister-in-law told me to feel free to do whatever I wanted. But then she kept saying, "Don't come near the refrigerator. Don't mess up the room." She would say, "Don't turn on the TV, I don't feel like watching now." She was always telling my kids, "No. No. No." She would tell my son, "Don't sit on the couch, you're going to get it dirty. Sit on the floor instead." In winter, she would sit in front of the heater and not give the kids a chance to go near it.

I couldn't say anything to her because it was her house. But the time there broke my son's heart. He was too shy to open the fridge and get something to eat. He felt pressured and put down. It was an ugly feeling. I was praying to God to have my own place. I dreamed to have my own TV that my kids could watch. If they asked me for their favorite food, I'd be able to cook it for them and no one would tell me, "No, we're cooking something else today."

⌒

THEY KEPT bombing everywhere. I took my kids from one place to another. We fled to one town, but they started bombing. We fled to another town, and they started bombing there too. We suffered a lot.

I met some people who were traveling to Lebanon. I traveled with them. We left together and got to the Bekaa Valley. Life in the camps was very difficult. We lived in a tent and there was no sanitation or hygiene. There was dirt everywhere. If someone got injured, the wound would become infected. My daughter got sick because it was impossible to keep her clean.

Someone mentioned the Widows Center. I applied and was accepted. I came to see what it was like to live here but was very scared. How am I going to deal with the people there? They were total strangers to me.

I came with nothing. Then one woman came to me and gave me a cup and a plate. It was lunchtime, and she filled the plate for me. She welcomed me and hugged me. In the evening, she came back to see if I needed anything.

Then the other women came to see me, one by one. The next morning, they were having breakfast together. They told me, "You're new here, come and have breakfast with us."

"You don't have a laundry basket, take this one."

"Your kids don't have clothes, take these."

They invited us downstairs, where they had school and activities. They helped the kids with their homework. They took them swimming and on field trips.

I felt great relief. I arrived very broken and started to feel strong. When I put my head on the pillow, I felt safe.

⌒

TODAY, I'M not the same person I used to be. When I got married, I never said "no" to anyone. I used to say "yes" to everything, even if it was at my own expense. Now I say, "This is my right, and this is your right." When I came here, my daughter was two years old. Now she is six years old, but she looks older than her age. She became strong and can protect herself. She says "no" for the things she doesn't like or "This is bothering me" or "I don't want that."

My son is ten years old now. He can watch whatever he wants on TV. There's no one to tell him, "No." Here, he can take a shower or have his favorite food. I take him out whenever I want. There's no one to tell me, "Wait, don't go." That's the difference between being stable or not. We have our own room. I can protect my kids and defend them. My kids draw their strength from my strength.

SOMETIMES, I wish I'd hear my phone ring. I become so excited when it rings, but it turns out to be just a friend. I have no one else left. If your parents are still alive, you visit them. But I have no brother, no uncle, no brother-in-law. No one is calling to see how I'm doing.

I always remember my house in Syria. I still love it. I feel that it's a piece of my heart. But it's too early to go back to Syria. You trust something only once. If it betrays that trust, you can't just trust again. If we went back, they would take our sons to war. I always think of myself as holding my son's hand with a tight grip. What would happen if I suddenly let go in the middle of the road?

This is my home now. No matter where I go or what I do, this will continue to be my home. We used to be terrified of the unknown, but not anymore. Our future is still uncertain, but we're not just sitting and waiting. We go for what we want, without fear. We have the strength to take risks. I will make sure my kids accomplish the things that I couldn't do in my life. I will no longer cry over the past.

Here is where I found safety, warmth, and tenderness. When I leave the Center, I feel that people are different from me. Inside the Center, we share the same wound. All of us here are one hand and we help each other. We remember our husbands and the lives we used to have.

The war and escaping and everything else that happened . . . We have become who we are today because of the great pain we suffered. Pain. Pain. And being told "No" or "You can't do that." That's what made us strong. Now we stand on our own feet. Now we are the ones who say, "No."

Fatima

I was in a very bad mental state and couldn't focus on anything. When I was working at Akilah Hospital, peoples' stories became too much for me to handle. When people feel that you sympathize with them and listen to their story, they tell you everything. I'd write down everything the patients told me. I still have that notebook, messy and torn.

I couldn't understand how life turned out like this. I couldn't understand what I was doing in this world. Why am I here? Why is there so much pain? Finally, the people at Akilah realized that I shouldn't be doing that job.

I was penniless and had to find new work. I'd go for long walks, sometimes walking for hours, aimlessly. Amman is mountainous, and I'd do up hills and down hills, and just walk and walk. I'd take unknown paths. If I got lost, I'd have to walk a lot to get back home because I didn't have enough money for transport. I'd walk and think, "Why is happiness on one side of things while Syrians are on the other side? Why is no one else like us?" I'd go to this park where people take photographs for engagements or graduations or events like that. Everyone there still felt that life is about celebrations, successes, dreams. I'd look at them and feel that we Syrians were different from the whole rest of the world.

(ɔ)

I HEARD about an American news organization giving media courses. I went and started training. The managers were mostly American. The instructors came from different countries. I thought that these people were definitely spies. I couldn't grasp that I was training at a nice place and was going to be paid for it too.

They had an English website and were setting up an Arabic site. The director knew through my Facebook page that my Arabic was very strong. They hired me to translate stories from English. The work was very stressful, but it was the best thing that ever happened to me. Translating news stories, I discovered that there was a lot that I didn't know about my own country. I didn't know about Syria's different regions. I heard about the Kurds and thought, "Were they really living among us?" I was clueless.

That period was very good for me. I worked with Syrians who understood what I was going through. I was living outside Syria but communicating with people inside Syria. I was writing about my country's news, and that made me very proud.

There were others in the team who didn't know the dark side of life. I met Americans with worlds of their own. I had new experiences that made me stronger. I'd ask someone, "What's your religion?" He'd say, "Irreligious." I thought, "What does 'irreligious' mean?" There was one friend I really liked who was very shy and sweet. And then she transitioned to become a man. That was something that I couldn't understand. According to my religion, God said, "We created you from a male and a female." But this person was very decent. Very sensitive, very smart, very loyal. I couldn't hate her. I told her, "It's hard for me to make the shift in Arabic from addressing you in the masculine form rather than the feminine form. But I will try. You've treated me with nothing but respect. I can do nothing but treat you the same way."

I made a lot of American friends. I'd see them smiling, reading, dreaming, thinking of the future. There was a guy named Dan. Once I asked him, "Dan, can I ask you a question?" He said, "Could you wait just one minute?" My God! He had everything calculated down to the minute! An airplane or missile could have ended my family's lives any-time. How could my whole life mean nothing, while a minute meant so much to him? This helped me want to dream again and think ahead. I thought, "Life is meaningful." Life wasn't only how it was on the Syrian side of things.

Ghani

AMMAN, JORDAN

I lived with my mom's relatives in Jordan for two months, but they couldn't cope with me. I don't blame them. When I saw anyone dressed in uniform, I started to scream. I'd also scream in the middle of the night. Once, my cousin woke up and saw me just standing in front of the wall. In prison, we used to stand up all night. That affected me for a long time.

My mom's family called her and said, "You need to come and get your crazy son." She took my disabled sister with her and came. We lived in Jordan for three and a half years. It was a hard life. The government didn't give us legal permits to work, but I had to find a job to take care of my mom and sisters. I worked under another barber and received just a percentage of what I earned. I got a lot of customers, but never felt safe. If the Jordanian government found me working, they'd put me in prison. I still felt that Syrian hands were trying to catch me and I was on the run.

I registered with the UN to be resettled in another country. They accepted to move my disabled sister and me to the UK. When we arrived at the airport in London, I felt, "I'm in a safe place now. I can breathe." Because we came through the UN, they provided us with a home, basic things, and a caretaker for my sister. They gave me an iPad to translate from Arabic to English. The first thing I did was lock the iPad in the cupboard. I told the caretaker, "Just explain to me with body language, and I'll explain to you with body language."

I'd go to the kitchen, bring a spoon, and say, "What do you call this in English?" She'd say "Spoon." I wrote it all down in my notebook: spoon, knife, fork . . .

On the third day, I walked to town on my own, did shopping on my own, and caught the bus back on my own. I came home and sat in the corner. And on that day, I decided to leave the past behind me and become a new person. Abdulghani is a person who was destroyed and broken. I choose a new future, a new life as a strong person, and a new name: Ghani.

ꙮ

IN SIX months, I started to speak to people in English. I went to the college. The lady said that they couldn't accept me in the barbering course because my English wasn't good enough.

I said, "My future is in your hands now. If you refuse me in your class, you will destroy me again. I have sixteen years of experience as a barber. Please just give me a chance."

She said, "What about your English?"

I said, "I'm a good learner. Just give me a chance."

And she did. I did barbering classes during the day and English classes in the evening. When I got back home at night, I looked after my sister and prepared her food. After she went to bed, I studied. I wrote words in my notebook: book, cat, moustache, eyebrows, whatever. I learned not just language but also the culture and lifestyle. On Fridays, they eat fish and chips. On Christmas, mince pie.

I felt that I needed to learn. I needed to be strong and independent. I had no time to waste. My English improved. I passed the first and the second year. I got my barber's diploma and found a job. My teacher recommended me, and I got certified to become a barbering teacher too.

I'd go on Instagram, Facebook, and YouTube, looking for new hairstyles, products, colors, and skin treatments. People come to me with messy hair or a messy beard. I change them from A to B. Gel and wax and they'll be handsome. Or they come in with normal skin, normal hair, nothing special. After a half an hour, they look in the mirror and—

"Wow!" That gives me a sense of "Yes! I did something." I love to put my signature on it. This is my passion. I can't do everything in this life, but I know how to be a barber. I know how to give people a new look. A good look.

The sky's my limit. I would like to learn every day, forever. I would like to be a successful person. I see myself one day on TV talking about refugees' experiences. About how we change and challenge ourselves. About how we face our problems and solve them. My dream is to make an academy for refugees: Ghani Academy. We'll teach the specific words that people need for barbering and makeup, and also for construction, cooking, and things like that. As refugees, we have a language barrier. In my academy, we'll try to give them the keys to find a job easily, without having to go to college for years. When you're interested in something, you pick up the words quickly. My aim is to help the refugee community be independent and confident. To say, "I'm a refugee and proud." My aim is to change views about refugees. We're not just coming to live off your taxes. We're human like you.

Now, when I speak Arabic, I speak in a tongue that isn't mine. I feel that it's Abdulghani who speaks. He is broken, with a lot of trauma and bad memories. But that's not me. I created a new person with new goals and new hope. I am Ghani, who builds himself. What the UK did was not just resettlement. It created me again. Yes, I worked hard for it too. But the UK gave me a chance. I belong to the UK because it treated me like a human when my homeland did not. England is not paradise, don't get me wrong. But this is my home. Here, I found what I didn't find in Syria or Jordan. I found love. Here, I can work hard and achieve things. Not just "I can." I will.

Alaa

HOMBURG, GERMANY

I remember one date while I was in detention with Military Security: June 18th. That was the day I was supposed to receive my high school diploma. That day, I isolated myself in the cell and exploded into tears. I cried through the night. Those feelings teach you: Syria is where you put in so much effort but lose so much. It's not the country you love, miss, and return to. Now I understand why a lot of Syrians my age in Germany learned to hate Syria. I understand them completely. Erase anything called Syria from your thoughts and look forward.

I didn't have expectations for life in Germany. I was in a refugee shelter for three months and then moved to an apartment with housemates. Then I moved to an apartment on my own. I've been in this same apartment for five years now. I have my own room, and this room is paradise for me. Every item was placed here by my own hands. I don't need more than this.

I learned the language slowly. I secluded myself completely and just studied, studied, studied, both in school and at home. I'd watch videos on YouTube. I'd buy a drink and read everything that was written on the label. I advanced through the levels and was accepted to a language course at the university. I wasn't actually a university student, but I was studying at the university. That was a dream for me.

I passed all the exams and started applying to universities in Germany. I applied to twenty-two universities in twenty-two cities. I printed my high school exam results twenty-two times and sent twenty-two envelopes with twenty-two stamps. I put all the money that I received as a refugee toward translating the required paperwork.

One university invited me to an interview. They asked, "Where do you see yourself in five years? How do you describe your personality? Tell us about a mistake you've made." In Syria, we were never taught questions like that. They sent me a very polite rejection and I hung it on the wall. I was proud of it. I wanted to reply to them: "Thank you for this rejection. Next time, I'll practice and improve."

I STARTED working at Burger King. The manager was also an immigrant and knew what it felt like. She insisted that I work at the cash register so I could interact with customers and practice my German. She believed that I could do it.

I worked there for two and a half years. I'd work long hours but didn't even feel it. The manager said that I was a hard worker and that it was good that I was in front because I smiled more than Germans do. Once a customer said, "We buy from him because he's always smiling." I felt like my effort was reciprocated. Those days were really beautiful for me. It wasn't like Syria, where you work for fifty years and then disappear in a second.

Later I got a second part-time job at a classy Italian restaurant. People who go to Burger King are generally working-class, because you can buy a meal for two euros. At the Italian restaurant, I'd see people in suits and ties paying ten euros for a salad. A salad! I was introduced to both sides of Homburg, the rich and the poor.

It's easy to get derailed in Germany. You don't have family to tell you what's right and wrong. If someone doesn't have a goal, they can get introduced to drugs. But I always had my dad's voice in my head: "We expect something great from you." I was working toward a goal and worked hard, like a horse with blinders.

AFTER A year, I again applied to all the dental schools in Germany. In Homburg, I also applied to medical school. I was accepted. I switched to part-time at Burger King and did extra hours on holidays or breaks. Sometimes during the semester, the manager would say, "I'll send you your paycheck. Stay home until you finish your exams."

That's how I spent my time. If I wasn't studying, I was working. The third semester was anatomy. It was really, really hard. I still don't understand how I survived that class. There were all these terms in Latin. We had oral exams, exams in morgues, exams on cadavers. I failed the first exam, so there was a lot of pressure to do well on the second and third exams. I would stay up at night, overthinking. The stress was like the stress I struggled with when I was in prison.

To qualify for a scholarship, you needed to have volunteer experience. I signed up for volunteer work translating for refugees and immigrants who were looking for apartments. I'd make appointments, read the contract to them, explain to them about the electricity, the utilities, water. "Keep in mind that you must inform the landlord three months before you vacate the apartment..." All of these details were totally new to us. The older generation had a lot of trouble with the new system. We in the younger generation could adapt. Our brains can be trained to learn new things.

෧

I'D PROMISED my dad that I would get my high school diploma and go to university. I wish he could be released from prison and see where I am today.

For three years, I was under siege or in prison or moving from house to house in Syria or in Germany. I didn't have anywhere to call home. Now Germany is home. When I settled here, I thought, "I'm staying." Homburg is my city. When I'm on the train and they call the stops and say, "Next stop, Homburg," I think, "I can't wait to get home." After years working at restaurants, I know a lot of people. Now no one can walk down the street with me, because I stop and say hi to all the people I know. A ten-minute walk turns into thirty minutes.

In Homburg, I know people from Portugal, Italy, Germany, Turkey, even Syria. They know I come from war, but not the full story. Two years ago, one of my sisters made it to Germany. Seeing her again for the first time was overwhelming. I'd been here alone, between two worlds. I was in Germany, speaking German, living a German lifestyle. When my sister came, I spoke Arabic and experienced an Arab environment. To sit with a sibling after four years is indescribable. You can't understand those beautiful details if you haven't lived them. We talked until the early hours of the morning. The sun rose, and we were still talking.

Houda

KHARTOUM, SUDAN

It's hard always being a stranger. When I visit family in the Gulf, I'm Syrian. When I visit family in the US, I'm a girl with a hijab. Here in Sudan, they call anyone with light skin "Halabi." So I'm Halabi.

It's hard feeling like you're not a part of something. Once I was walking down the street in Khartoum and saw a funeral gathering. After the burial, people sit in a tent, recite the Quran, and drink coffee. I saw that and started to cry. Not because it was a funeral, but because everybody there knew each other. They're all relatives or neighbors.

My mom says, "I just want to go back to Syria and walk the streets." I don't have those feelings anymore. I want to remember Syria the way it was when I last saw it. Syria is so different now. Most of the people I knew are no longer there, and the ones there have changed. I've changed too. We've all changed. I want to keep Syria as the place of my memories until I'm ready to go back and do something to alleviate the misery.

I love Sudan. I'm happy, but I know it's temporary. When you think of a place as temporary, it can't feel like home. Any time I buy something new, I think, "How will I pack this when I leave?" This is a Syrian thing. You're always packing.

There's another Syrian thing: "Holiday Zoom call." You have family all over the place, so this is how we can see each other. Three years ago, we actually gathered as a family for my cousin's wedding. It had been seven years since I'd seen my whole family together. My uncle did a lot of work to get all my aunts out of Syria.

My siblings and I were little when we left Syria. Now we're young adults. My brothers have beards and stuff. One of my aunts asked my sister, "Who are you?" When my sister said her name, my aunt started crying. Every single one of my aunts cried when they saw us again.

☙

IN THE fourth year of medical school, they took about sixty of us female students to spend twenty-one days in a village on the Nile. They told us, "If later you want to be a doctor in rural areas or refugee camps, you have to learn how to deal with difficulties."

That's where I saw the real Sudan, not like my apartment in Khartoum. The sixty of us stayed in this house with a dirt floor. There were no electrical lights at first, but then people in the village worked to hook some up. We got water from a simple faucet outside. The walls were covered with spider webs. It was the first time I'd seen something like this. The hospital had no equipment. If you're injured and go to the doctor, you have to bring your own suture and needle and everything else you need. Once, we had an open day at the clinic; about a hundred and fifty patients came, and more than half had malaria.

They have a mosque and something called *khalwa*, like a school where they teach Islamic knowledge. There were three hundred students from all over Sudan, aged five to eighteen. They memorize the Quran by writing with charcoal on wooden boards. We thought, "Oh, poor kids! They're away from their families. They have nothing." We gave the kids toothbrushes and taught them basic things, like if you touch something dirty and then eat with your hands, you might get sick.

Then the older kids said that they wanted us to listen to them. They gathered us in a room and recited some Quran for us. They were so polite. Their eyes were filled with respect. I don't know how to put it. Their recitation, their voices . . . they felt every single letter of what they were saying. They were so pure. It's like they had never seen anything bad in this world. Nothing distorted their innocence.

I've memorized the Quran and listened to the Quran all my life. But when I heard certain verses from their voices, it felt like I was hearing them for the first time. There are moments in my life when I've really felt like a Muslim. This was one of them.

All sixty of us medical students left crying. For the next hour, we just sat under the trees, silent. We no longer felt sorry for those kids. We felt sorry for ourselves. I had felt sorry for the kids because they had no connection to the rest of the world. But then I started to feel sorry for myself because I was so connected to the world. They had a connection to something greater. I was really humbled. At that moment, I knew what I wanted on a spiritual level. You think, "I don't want anything else."

I hope that everyone has an experience like this. I'm grateful that I came to Sudan. People ask me, "How did you choose Sudan?" I always say, "I didn't choose Sudan. Sudan chose me." It hasn't been easy at all. But I don't think I would be the same person if I hadn't come here. There are moments, especially when you're young, when you think, "Why I'm doing this? What's the point of it all?" Being a Muslim gives me answers, but sometimes you need a reminder. Sudan is a reminder that will have a long-term effect on me. Before I came to Sudan, I was doing things just because I had to. Now I have reasons. I'll do the same things, but now with a different mindset and purpose.

Nour

The university was in Ankara, far from where my family settled in Mersin. I lived away from my family for the first time. The city was huge. And the university was very liberal.

It was a shock. My mom is religious and traditional, but also feminist in her own way. She'd always planted in me the idea that I'm a smart Muslim girl. My role is to show the world that Muslim women can be religious and also be successful in life. In Syria, I did well in school, was in Girl Scouts, and had a circle of friends who were also smart girls. I started wearing a hijab at a young age. My parents were happy that I never had rebellious teenage years.

When I was growing up, everything made sense. I had Syria. I had home. I was making my family proud. I was doing things for the right reasons: for God, my country, my culture. My religion, my family, the way I dressed; it all fit together. And then, suddenly, I was outside my home. The secular environment in Turkey challenged my beliefs, my role in life, my sense of belonging. People at the university started questioning all of my identities at the same time. Questioning the basis of my life, my whole being.

It was scary. If you're not *that* person, then who are you? I slowly started to build my own identity. My ideas changed. I kept reading, searching, and working on how I perceive myself and the world around me. I also thought about how I want others to see me. I remember one day I looked in the mirror and realized that I didn't know that girl wearing a hijab. It wasn't me. I had a kind of a breakdown for two weeks where I would get dressed and then start crying. I didn't want to leave home because I didn't feel comfortable in my own skin.

I wasn't sure why I was feeling this way. I thought that maybe if I lost weight, I'd be happy in my body again and all would be well. Unfortunately, I developed an eating disorder. I was hospitalized three times. It wasn't pretty. My mom came and took care of me, for which I'll be forever thankful. She was the support I needed. She made food and made sure I was eating well. Before she came, my little studio apartment didn't feel like home. But when my mom was there, she made a warm home for me. During that time in my life, home was wherever my mom was. I was still too young to link myself to a home of my own.

℗

I CAME to hate wearing the hijab. I realized that I was probably wearing it because of my family and the effect of my surroundings in Syria. But if I took it off, would it only be because of my surroundings at the university? I decided to wait until I graduated and didn't have that circle of people around me anymore. Then I could make the decision for myself.

I graduated and was offered a scholarship in Denmark. Denmark was a whole new chapter. Being secular in Turkey is different from being secular in Europe. Alcohol culture was quite a shock.

In an ideal world, even if you're dressed in a certain way, you won't be stereotyped. Unfortunately, we don't live in that world. Wearing the hijab, I would always be placed in a certain box. I didn't want all those judgments placed on my shoulders every time I met someone new. And I didn't want to wear hijab anymore, because that was no longer me.

So, I decided to take off my hijab. At first, I wasn't sure if I was doing it due to outside pressure or because this is actually who I am. After six months, I started to feel more comfortable in my skin. I also loved the freedom of not having to worry so much about dressing in a way to make people think that I'm a *modern* Muslim girl. As a girl with a hijab, you have to make extra effort because it's not easy to cover yourself from head to toe and still look chic. And that's not really my thing.

The first year in Denmark, there was a lot of trial and error in how I dressed. I felt like I was discovering myself. Do I like shorter dresses or longer dresses? Do I want to dress the way I used to or show more skin? I tried everything I could. I slowly realized that, even if I'm no longer wearing a hijab, I still don't want to use my body to get close to people. I went back to dressing modestly, but in an empowered way. It was nice realizing that this is who I am.

It really pains my mom that I'm not religious anymore. I understand. She wants the best for me and, for her, that means being religious. But I know myself. I'm in touch with my authentic self. And I'm much more content now than I ever was before.

Rifaie

When my wife went into labor, it was a mix of joy and trauma. Watching your loved one go through so much pain! At some point she said, "I can't push anymore." I said, "We've been training for this. You've been exercising every day. You can do it."

And then, at 11:10 p.m., our son was born. I was in shock; I just couldn't believe that everything was okay. I wanted to stay, but my wife and the baby needed rest so I went back home. I remember that it was three or four o'clock in the morning. I was on my way back home and suddenly my purpose in life became so vivid: I simply needed to do everything I could to protect my wife and my baby and make sure that we would always be together and safe.

We named our son Muhammad, or Hamoudi for short. We named him after my father, who had passed away in Syria. It was a way of paying tribute to him and preserving his legacy. My wife was the first to suggest this, but she was also worried that every time I looked at our son, I might have traumatic memories of my father. I said that this shouldn't be an issue. Instead, I think of my dad's courage and what he stood for: resisting, refusing to give up, refusing to leave. Now I imagine my dad watching over us. I hope that he'd be proud.

THE BEGINNING was really tough. Hamoudi wasn't a good sleeper. He didn't latch on properly to breastfeeding. My wife struggled, always wondering if she was doing the right thing. She struggled, and I struggled watching her struggle. I ended up dropping everything to stay at home. There was a point when I couldn't even leave home without fear for her.

The doctors said, "This is normal. All parents experience this." But I think it was more extreme for us because we didn't have any family support. My wife's family was in different states in Australia. My mom and sister were still in Turkey. Eventually, it got so bad that we decided to go to my family in Turkey rather than wait until I finished my Ph.D. later that year, as we'd originally planned. We were just in desperate need of help.

⊙

WHEN WE arrived in Gaziantep, I was so full of emotion that I was numb. It was the first time that I'd seen my mom and sister in seven and a half years. Due to visa restrictions, I was not able to visit before I became an Australian citizen. And then there was the pandemic, and borders closed. I left Turkey by myself as a twenty-seven-year-old and came back with a wife and baby. When I left, my sister Shahd was seven years old and less than half my height and size. I came back and she was fifteen and just a bit shorter than me.

We spent six weeks with them. The best thing was seeing the connection between Shahd, my mother, and Hamoudi. You could see the affection and unconditional love. It showed me what really matters in life. Is it my career? Is it being in an incredible country where living conditions are easier than elsewhere? Or is it considering what I might regret ten or twenty years from now? Everything just kind of nailed down the importance of family. The importance of proximity over everything else.

It wasn't until I got to Turkey that I told my mom that my applications to resettle her and my sister in Australia had been rejected. They'd been rejected long before that, but I didn't want to tell her until we were together. During all the time that I'd been away, she'd kept hoping that she would come to Australia someday. After we talked, she started to accept that it probably wouldn't happen. She'd been in Turkey for nine years in a furnished place but had never bought some things that she wanted because she thought she would be leaving soon. So, she finally started buying things. She bought a vacuum cleaner, a microwave, and this expensive set of couches. They were beautiful couches, and she was very happy with them.

WE WENT back to Australia. There had been support . . . and then suddenly there was none. And that's when things got worse for my wife. I raised the alarm to health services. Finally, she was diagnosed with postnatal depression.

Things eventually got better, but we still had to think about what we wanted. We're both Australian citizens and Australia is a great country. We love it. I speak the language and am used to everything. I've made friends and have a good network. We have good chances to build careers and build a life . . . just without my mom and sister.

My wife made the argument that we should go back to Turkey. She said that we should go back immediately, right after I finished my degree.

I said, "Let me at least apply for some jobs first."

She said, "You always say that family is the top priority. They can't travel, but we can. It's our duty to go to them."

I was like, "You're right." And I started continuing her sentences. I said, "We have flexibility. There's no excuse. Why don't we make the decision to be with them, and let everything else fall into place based on that?"

We agreed that we wanted my mom and sister to be present in Hamoudi's life. To play an active role in how he's raised culturally, religiously, socially, emotionally, psychologically, physically. So, we made this huge move. We bought tickets to leave twenty days later. We packed our stuff. We sold what we could and gave away what we couldn't.

We came to Turkey with a visa for three months. We plan to use this time to be with my mom and sister, and apply for jobs in Turkey, Europe, or the Gulf. If we don't find anything after three months, we'll move to another country. If I get a job in Europe, maybe we'll move there and come back to visit my mom and my sister monthly. Or maybe I'll be able to sponsor them to join us there.

Many people were shocked by our decision to leave Australia and move back to Turkey. My own relatives lectured me, "Australia is one of the most amazing countries on earth! Why would you leave heaven?" But we have a proverb in Arabic, "Heaven without people is not worth it." My mom in any country in the world is better than the best country in the world without her.

Our idea of home remains in flux because we still haven't found a place where we can all be together permanently. Australia is definitely *one* home. If my mom and sister were able to go to Australia, it could be *the* home. That would be where I would settle down, spread my roots, build a foundation, and really invest in a place. That is, have a home in the literal sense. Because that hasn't happened yet, we're still in limbo. I'm still trying to find that home that can house us all.

VI

BELONGING

GHADA, DUHA, RAJA,

SARA A., ASMA, MASRI, OKBA,

AHLAM, RIFAIE

Building home is a story that reaches inward into people's evolving sense of self and purpose. Belonging is a story that turns outward, anchoring home in the relationships that people develop with the physical and social worlds around them.

Definitions of belonging vary. For philosopher Linn Miller, belonging is a mode of being that integrates key aspects of the self.[1] Miller notes that people have varied connections to the contexts in which they live, such as social connections to communities, historical connections to the past, and geographical connections to particular localities. People belong when they believe that these or other connections are right and fitting, allowing them to live with integrity and authenticity. Belonging, in this view, is the special well-being that results when one is at ease with oneself and in accord with who one is in the world.

Belonging is a feeling, but not merely a feeling. It is also a question of power. Some theorists have conceptualized what they call the "politics of belonging" to describe how authority and resources structure how individuals or groups are accepted or denied membership in a larger collective.[2] Ties of belonging are thus also relationships of inclusion or exclusion, sometimes drawing boundaries between an "us" and a "them." For refugees and migrants, the politics of belonging is palpable when politicians or publics whip up anti-refugee sentiment, legal regimes deny basic rights and opportunities, or economic restrictions make it difficult to earn a dignified living. Power relationships can also infuse the more subtle ways that communities welcome or reject newcomers based on assumptions about who counts as a refugee deserving of solidarity or what appreciation host societies are owed.

The narratives in this section illustrate some of the complexities shaping both the emotions and the politics of belonging. The first three voices emphasize different kinds of belonging to Syria, Syrian culture, and Syrians as a people. They provide a window into how diasporas form as communities abroad that are uniquely linked to a common homeland. Ghada, still without information about the fate of her arrested husband, nurtures deep bonds with other relatives of disappeared persons in exile. She devotes herself to educating refugee children and encouraging their sense of belonging to the Syrian hometowns that they scarcely remember. Duha arrives in a Turkish border town feeling like a plant without soil. With time, she builds a new sense of belonging to the large Syrian community that is itself taking root there. In Berlin, Raja gathers a choir where Syrian women not only find their voices but also become family to each other and powerful bearers of their shared artistic heritage.

Others describe how they do or do not develop a sense of belonging in their new countries of settlement. Sara A. critiques the possessive connotations of the word "belonging," but relishes the points of connection that she uncovers in Brazil and how they resonate with emotional memories. Similarly far from large centers of Syrian diasporic life, Asma does not feel an immediate attachment to Tunisia. As she devotes effort to cultivating friendships and local knowledge, however, the country transforms into home. Still, just as Asma eventually brushes against the limits of belonging without legal security, Masri also finds that his search for stability remains elusive. After the brutal trek out of his besieged hometown leads him to internal displacement, refuge in Lebanon, and finally studies in Japan, he finds that he belongs to causes more than places. For Okba, alone during his first weeks in Bavaria, a sense of belonging to his new country of settlement also seems out of reach. He comes to regret the long journey that brought him to Europe—until a single greeting kicks off a succession of life-changing relationships.

Crises can reveal feelings and understandings of belonging in new ways, bringing to the fore both where one wants to be and who one can count on for support. Such was the case for millions of displaced Syrians affected by the devastating February 2023 earthquakes in Turkey and Syria.* Ahlam recalls living the earthquake from the Syrian side of the border. Amidst nearly indescribable destruction and death, she recommits her belonging to her homeland. Rifaie recalls his experiences from the Turkish side of the border, where he, his wife, and his baby had relocated after losing hope in the chance of resettling his mother and sister in Australia. His belonging remains to the four people most precious in his life, though he could not have imagined the turn of events that finally give them the chance to live together.

These narratives provide a window into the diverse ways that people define belonging, come to feel belonging, and relate to that to which they belong. They also illustrate the obstacles that can thwart such a sense of belonging, from precarious legal statuses to the daunting task of building friendships where everyone is a stranger. Cultivating belonging after displacement is a story of confronting these obstacles to develop meaningful connections with the worlds in which one lives. It can also demand grappling with how those worlds have transformed. For many who flee violence and persecution, belonging is thus a product of not only inclusion and affinity but also perseverance.

---

* On February 6, 2023, back-to-back magnitude 7.8 and magnitude 7.5 earthquakes struck near the border between Turkey and northwest Syria. The twin blasts and thousands of aftershocks affected some 16 million people, killing more than 55,000 and causing an estimated $34 billion in damage.

Ghada

For years, every day, I would read the last text that my husband sent me before he was arrested. That phone eventually broke, unfortunately. I wish that I still had it. Other women have some of their husbands' things, but I wasn't able to keep anything that belonged to him.

In 2016, I was invited to join a campaign organized by five women who also had loved ones in prison. From the beginning, it felt like family. We understand each other so well. We share the same pain. If I cry, they know why without me even saying it.

The group got a red bus from London and covered it with photos of detainees. We felt that we had to pay our respects to our heroes and get the world to pay attention. This was also something that we did to support ourselves, psychologically. I couldn't travel to see the bus because I didn't have a passport. But I saw the photos. I cried a lot when I saw my husband's picture. People also took the photos from the bus and held them. When we saw the man holding my husband's picture, my daughter said, "I want to kiss that man's hands."

☙

WHEN WE got to Lebanon, I enrolled my kids in school. I learned that most Syrian students were failing. People claim that Syrian refugees and Lebanese are being treated equally, but schools have two shifts: morning for Lebanese and evening for Syrians. By evening, Lebanese teachers are tired and don't teach Syrians properly. Also, Lebanese schools are English-based while Syrian schools are Arabic-based. Syrian kids weren't prepared.

I felt that we should start something of our own. I gathered some Syrians I knew to volunteer to teach supplemental classes. We did this for a year and then I met a priest. He believed in the project and gave me two thousand dollars. I bought tables and chairs and supplies and we kept going. Then another priest spoke with German donors who asked me to submit a proposal. They gave me a small amount to see how things went. We moved to a larger building and kept going. Later, they gave us a larger amount.

Now we have around four hundred students from kindergarten through eighth grade. We're going to start to take ninth grade too. We teach English, math, science. In the summer, we have activities. Every time we get more funds, we expand our ideas and try something new.

WE HAD twins in the kindergarten class. We asked where they are from and they said, "Ghazzeh, Lebanon." We said, "No, where are you from in Syria?" They started to yell, "We're not Syrian, we're Lebanese!" Their parents had taught them: if you ever get lost, tell people you're from Ghazzeh, so they bring you back.

I realized that we needed to educate our kids about Syria. In school, they're taught Lebanese geography and history. Parents just want their kids to succeed and don't want to add another topic on top of what they already study. But that means no one is teaching them about Syria. Now I understand how Iraqi refugees felt when they came to Syria and went to our schools. They had to study about Syria, even though they had their own country to belong to.

We decided to focus the last month of summer activities on belonging, heritage, and homeland. We brainstormed how language teachers could use writing assignments that asked kids to talk about their hometowns and villages, and what they're famous for. I attended the first class and had to hold back tears. One kid from Saqba said, "When you go back home, you should buy your furniture from us in Saqba." Another kid said, "We have furniture in Daraya too." A third kid said, "Our town is called Harran al-Awamid. Why does it have that name?" We are now planning a play where everyone talks about their hometowns, speaking in their local accent. It will reinforce the idea of belonging.

We drew a big map of Syria on the floor and students had to identify heritage sites. They knew the capital and all fourteen Syrian governorates. We talked about traditional clothes and did some traditional songs and dances. We told them that the first alphabet in the world came from Syria. We talked about poets and Zenobia, the queen of Palmyra who fought the Romans. I showed a student a picture of the suspension bridge in Deir ez-Zor, and he thought it had to be in the United States.

Our kids didn't know any of this before. They always feel down because back home there is war and here they're strangers. Lebanese kids think that they're better than Syrian kids. They think that Syrian kids are dirty. That they live in camps and beg on the streets. We want to show our kids that Syria is a beautiful country. We want them to be proud of their home.

Duha

When we got to Reyhanlı, I was broken. I felt like a plant that was cut and placed in a cup of water. If it sprouts roots, they don't grow into earth.

We said that we didn't need to buy furniture, that we'd sleep on simple mattresses until we went back. We told Turkish landlords that we wouldn't pay a full year's rent because we'd be returning to Syria in two months. And those two months turned into ten years. You felt like you were at the start of a very dark tunnel. You're tied to a boulder and you're pulling, pulling, pulling. You don't know when you'll find the exit.

We found an apartment building with seventeen units. We were relatives and we rented all of them. During Ramadan, it's custom for everyone to give everyone else a dish of what they cooked. We did that so we wouldn't feel like anything was different. In the evening, we spread a tablecloth on the floor of the common area and sat together, drinking tea and chatting. For the holiday, we made the cookies that are part of our history. I'm sure you can buy cookies that taste better, but these are cookies that we make with our own hands and they're connected to a special memory.

We created a strong identity as the Syrian community in Turkey. It's a hard-working community. The majority of the population in Reyhanlı now is Syrian. Everything there looks different from when we first arrived. When you see a Turk on the street, you think, "What are you doing here?"

◎

WHEN PEOPLE migrate, they try to recreate the places where they come from. But we have this saying: "You can take me back to the same old café, but can you also give me the old friends who I used to know there?" A place is really the people you know and love. Friends are what determine if you feel *ghurba* or not. I belong first and foremost to Syria but, with time, my sense of belonging has instead become to Syrians. I can leave a place. As long as I have people with me, we can create a shared identity, culture, and tradition wherever we are.

I also feel belonging to my pen. When I have a pen and paper, no one can prevent me from exercising my rights. I might never go back to Syria in my lifetime. But through my writing, I document my love and belonging to that place. I create something that future generations might read. They can know that this place existed. That it was our land, where our families planted cucumbers, eggplants, and tomatoes. Where we ate food fresh from the oven.

I try to do things that remind me of that place. The house that I live in now has a terrace and I planted flowers there. It transports my sense of belonging. It reminds me of where everything was green. Where, during the harvest season, you smelled the smell of grain mixed with the smell of the soil and the people. I'm nostalgic for that place, where there were simple people with simple dreams. Nothing can compare to the feeling of peace watching the sunset there. I wish that my kids will have experiences like that.

Raja

A rt and culture can create knowledge and bring change. It slowly stirs what is inert. It can make you realize how valuable you are.

This is my mission in society. In Arab countries, there's a view that people over fifty should just stay at home. Their lives are finished, especially if they're women. In 2010, I started a project in Damascus: a music group for elderly men and women called the Renaissance Choir. Some members were over eighty. With group singing, you don't need to have a good voice. You get the chance to sing and that makes you happy.

Everyone thought of the first song that they loved and what it meant to them. Then we'd all learn the song and sing it together. People would go home singing and sing the whole rest of the week. At the next rehearsal, they would learn a new song and that would stick with them for the rest of the week too. Once a lady called me. She said, "I'm not going to tell you who I am, but I want to thank you. My mother-in-law has always been grumpy. Now she is singing all the time. You're doing great work."

◎

I SUPPORTED the revolution. I saw the regime as disgusting, corrupt filth. As human beings, we deserve to be treated better. We deserve a homeland.

We took part in a public conference demanding the change of the regime. After that, there were many arrests, so we left. My husband found a job in the UAE and then Qatar. But I felt very ill at ease. I couldn't remain far away.

I went to the Turkish-Syrian border. I saw poverty and misery. Syrian women had lost their husbands and children. Some had children in jail. I told them, "Let's sing."

They said, "We can't sing!"

I said, "Let's try."

I hired a trainer. Women laughed and said I was crazy, but they came. Half an hour later, they were so happy. It was their first time singing. They flushed away the misery that they had been living for five years. They jumped, shouted, ululated. I'd known that they would enjoy it. I had experience with this. And in my mind, art is always the solution.

Later, I came to Germany. I reached out to women from the choir who had also come to Germany. I suggested that we get together and sing. The group in Turkey continues. The group in Germany currently has seventeen members, though double that number have come and gone over the years. We practice weekly. We held events in a nursing house and a hospice center. We did concerts at museums and the international book festival.

In Turkey, I met people from every part of Syria and collected their traditional songs. Syria was always divided, and people from different regions didn't really mingle with each other. Now I have built enough of a collection of songs that we have concerts that travel through the south, middle, north, and coastal regions of Syria. In one concert, you feel as though you visited the whole country.

Membership is open to everyone. We target women over fifty, but many young women come too. Usually, young women don't like to spend time with old ones. They make fun of these traditional songs about innocent love and things like that. But now young people are interested. I think that they're trying to preserve their Syrian identity. No other reason could make young people come and sing these songs. It's an indication of how valuable their heritage is to them. They took our houses and country. They took away the jasmine of Damascus. But our musical heritage is part of our memories and consciousness. No one can take that away.

We're making families for these young people. I often find one of the young women leaning her head on my shoulder. I pat their heads and cook for them. Such an atmosphere makes them feel at home. They feel a need to be with their mothers, but their families are scattered. We offer each other affection and support. In Turkey, the daughter of one woman in the choir was getting married. When a girl marries, usually aunts, uncles, and grandparents come to visit. As this woman had no one there, the choir was her family. We came and sang some songs. We danced and cheered for her. Just yesterday here in Berlin, one woman was sick and eight of us went to check on her. It is our custom to bring a gift when you visit, so each of us pitched in five euros to buy her something. She was so happy. If we were not in the music group, none of us would even know each other.

I believe that change will start like this, from the bottom up. The women who come to rehearse work beautifully as a team. They sing together, breathe together. Together, they feel powerful. They now have this experience of being able to gather and do something. We can be the women who bring peace to Syria. We are waiting for that opportunity.

Sara A.

SÃO PAULO, BRAZIL

When I was in Egypt, Egyptian trade union activists introduced me to Brazilian trade unionists. We met and started exchanging ideas. Then I was contacted by a trade union federation in Brazil that had an internationalist perspective. They were connected with South Africa, the Middle East, various places. They said, "Why don't you come to Brazil?"

I came to Brazil with a program. I went from one city to another and from one state to another. We translated documentaries about Syria into Portuguese and showed them all over the place. I was this random Syrian talking to people who couldn't locate Syria on the map. I visited urban and rural occupations on the verge of being expelled. I visited twenty federal universities, where we would have very academic debates. The same day, they'd take me to a school where I'd face fifty twelve-year-olds.

The geopolitical consciousness of what the Middle East is—the construction of the Middle East as Europe's "other"—didn't exist in Brazil. I had to speak to people as comrades: as people who listen. I had to say, "You know how the military police enters your house and destroys everything on top of your head? Imagine if this happened to you every day..." I had to find ways to speak without making it specific to Syria. That was beautiful, because we tend to be very Syria-centric, and I hate that.

This was at a time when the Syrian revolution was in the phase of writing proposals and asking for grants. It felt like we had to prove that we were worthy of being invested in. Here in Brazil, it just wasn't like that. At the end of every talk, we'd say, "We are trying to raise funds to support a local governance council in liberated parts of Syria. It doesn't matter how much you give." People had no intention of showing any kind of superiority through philanthropy. You went to a farmer and a teacher, and they would donate three *reals* because they felt solidarity with people they knew nothing about.

That had a profound influence on me. I felt that I had done everything that I could do in the Middle East and was in a new place where I could see a new horizon. I started participating in picket lines and going to assemblies. It was a world that was so distant to me and so inspiring. That was what pulled me in. I wanted to be here because of this. I could see a future where I could connect with people.

This was also the time when everybody was being counted. There was this terminology of "waves" of migrants and refugees. Waves and waves. It seemed like something with so little agency. I needed a collective project where I would be able to fight not only for Syria but also for causes on a much wider scale. I didn't feel that I could find this project in Europe or the United States. I wanted to be south. And this is why Brazil means so much to me. After losing our house in Syria, home became a need for me. I came to Brazil and saw that there is beauty everywhere. I knew that this is where I wanted to be.

⌒

TO ME, home has always been the people around me and the memories I have with them. Now, home is equally where I can walk down the street and have various types of relationships—with the bakery on the corner, with the guy who sells corn on the street, with the crazy neighbor who I sometimes fight with because she plays music too loud.

Home is a place where I can imagine raising children, whether or not I want children. I would want to raise children with the values and challenges that might be brought into their life in Brazil. Home is a place where I feel that I can connect with others without being "otherized" so much. I live in São Paolo, one of the most dangerous cities in the world. If I walk downtown there might be a pickpocket, but there isn't violence in people's eyes that says, "Who are you? Are you from here? Are you from somewhere else?"

This othering process creates so much animosity. But there's no single "type" in Brazil. You see so many kinds of people, so many different cultures, from the Indigenous to the Italian to the Afro-Brazilian. I like that it's not easy to categorize people. It's funny because, when I speak Portuguese with my bit of accent, they think I'm Argentinian. They're like, "Ahh! Argentina!" So even when they see you as a stranger, it's fun.

South America has been through its share of violent colonialism and dictatorships. Brazilians had their own experience of military dictatorship very recently. And in the process of democratization, none of those leaders really ever went to jail. All this makes it easier to discuss pain and suffering and the contradictions of living it. It gives you common ground to work from. It's very eye-opening to be able to have a comparative experience on people, regimes, everything—but without saying "we suffered more than you did." For me, exile has been a liberation from nationalism, even on a sentimental level. I'm forever grateful for that. You become more humble. You see yourself in others and others in yourself.

☙

I'M SOMEONE who makes a home anywhere I go. I think it's a need. Anywhere I go, I sort of shoot roots. When I go to Airbnbs, I put a vase of flowers next to my bed. My house in São Paulo has the strong feel of somebody who is not simply passing through. My plants are here, my books, my photos, my smells, my experiences.

All of this means a lot to me. But it's not about belonging in the sense of making the house mine. The word "belonging" doesn't resonate with me. It's just not my frame of reference. It sounds too possessive. Like any word, it has a certain amount of baggage. Like being stuck in the ground. Like, are you here? Or are you there?

Be-long—being and longing, you know? Maybe the longing goes back to nostalgia. I'm critical of nostalgia sometimes because I've seen how the idea of a golden age can be employed politically. I don't like looking back and staying there. If I feel nostalgia, I need to do something with it. Cooking is very nostalgic for me. I like searching for ingredients to recreate the dishes I grew up with. I like studying with the guy at the farmer's market about whether this or that herb might work for a particular dish.

I love the feeling of being nostalgic and sharing it with people. Once, we did an event called a *sarao*, which was a kind of poetry reading and discussion of feminism. I thought, "Let's do it in a way that's a bit more Syrian." I remember seeing my mom using henna with her friends and sisters. Applying henna and taking care of the body was very much a social act back in Syria. So I made the *sarao* a henna party. I invited twenty girls over to my house and prepared gigantic bowls of henna. We had tea and they brought poetry, and it was sort of an Audre Lorde thing. It was really beautiful.

There is a flower that blooms at night and has a beautiful smell. In Brazil, they call it "Lady of the Night." In Syria, we call it "Light of the Night." I love that I walk down the street here and inhale that scent. I live near a samba school. When they train for Carnival, you hear the voice of the head of the school on the microphone. I live in a valley, so the sound echoes from a distance. In the beginning, I couldn't hear exactly what he was saying. To me, it was just a call from far away. Sometimes when I dozed off, I could swear that it was a mosque's call to prayer.

These parallels are emotional and exhilarating, but without the feeling, "We will return to Syria." No. Maybe we won't return. But that doesn't mean I lose the power of these beautiful experiences.

IN SYRIA, somebody was always knocking on the door and coming over. There's lunch prepared for four people and ten people show up. The idea of family and friends and friends of family was always like this in Syria. When I lived in Beirut, I had roommates or later my sister joined me at the university. In Egypt, it was bubbling with revolution, so we always had people over too.

When I first arrived in São Paolo and didn't have that kind of dynamic in the house, I got a bit depressed. It was lonely. My house was too quiet. That's how the dogs came into my life. When I was younger in Syria, I was scared of dogs. I knew nothing about them. But here I thought, "Let's find a cute little thing that can make noise and bring some life to the house." They made all the difference. I gave the first one a name in Portuguese that can be Arabized. I thought, "You never know. Maybe I'll take him back to Lebanon or Syria." So I called him Jose, which is Youssef in Arabic. When I'm talking to him in a friendly way, I call him "Zé." But when I shout at him, I yell, "Yousef!"

Asma

TUNIS, TUNISIA

There are people who you click with right away and people whose relationships need work. For me, Istanbul was love at first sight. In Tunis, I had to put effort into finding things I enjoyed. After a while, I understood that I was not going to connect with the whole city directly and instinctively. I needed to look for little things to connect with. I made a conscious decision to search and read and give it more time. Slowly, I built a very good connection with the city. Not as a whole package, but through places, activities, and small stuff. I put those things together and was able to create my own tie to the place.

❧

THERE ARE so many beautiful details. For example, jasmine is everywhere. Huge, huge trees of jasmine. Damascenes always love to talk about the jasmine of Damascus. But Tunisians' relationship with jasmine is a whole culture. They make something called *mashmoom*. Wherever you go in the summer, people are selling it on the streets. They get up very early to pick jasmine flowers and tie their stems together in a little bouquet. You can put it in your hair or your car or your home, and you smell jasmine all the time. I heard that, back in the day, *mashmoom* was kind of like Tinder: if a guy likes a girl, he gives her *mashmoom*. If she has the *mashmoom* in her hair on the right, it means that she is already with somebody. If she puts the *mashmoom* on the left, it means she's available.

There are so many little things in Tunisia. I spent so much time in the Old Medina and created my network. I know somebody who makes perfume oils. I know a lady who brings couscous with the original grain all the way from this town and the guy who gets dried octopus from that town. I became friends with a guy who makes leather bags, and every time I go to the Medina, we have tea together. Eventually, my Tunisian friends would ask me, "Where do we go for this or that?"

The house I lived in became my home. I cooked and hosted feasts. I held weekly movie nights and would invite people. Sometimes twenty people attended and sometimes only one person showed up. For about two years, I put in effort. Then, I forgot that it was effort. I just got into the rhythm and went with the flow.

I learned to speak the Tunisian dialect of Arabic. I listened and tried to say things and somehow it came to me. I had a friend who moved to the neighborhood, and then friends of his also moved in. We had three apartments in the same area, and we became really close to each other. During the Corona lockdowns, we'd go to the roof of their building and hang out the whole weekend. This made my relationship with the country even stronger. I learned about the politics, the people, the history. I watched these videos that you'd only know about from locals and got to know all this funny slang.

It's a huge shift to go from knowing absolutely nothing about a country to having a family. I never felt non-Tunisian. I never had this feeling, "Oh, you're not from here." I had a different experience, and that was seen and appreciated. But I never felt like I was treated as "not one of us." I was just there. I was accepted. I belonged, really belonged. Now Tunisia is my comfort zone. It's home for me.

@

I DON'T think home is simply a place, because places change. Often, I link home with foods or smells, and sometimes with music. My dad used to play Iraqi songs in the morning. For me, that was home. Now listening to Tunisian music is also home for me. It brings back a fragment of a memory of feeling comfortable. A moment when you felt at ease.

Sometimes it's the sun. In my village in Syria, there's a specific type of cold you feel in winter. It's dry, but sunny. I remember feeling that kind of cold once in the mountains in northwest Tunisia. I felt the sun and the temperature of the air. My face was cold, but not so cold. I thought, "Oh God, this reminds me of home." It wasn't the place. It was more like a feeling.

It took time and effort to make Tunisia home. I could have stayed, but I needed something more stable—a base where I could say, "This is where I am. This is where my stuff is. I can move and I can come back." In Tunisia, my residency papers were dependent on work. I didn't have the luxury of quitting my job or taking some time off or not having a plan. There was nothing called freedom of movement. And Tunisia couldn't give me options for the future. I needed to get somewhere that could give me papers. Having a Syrian passport is like carrying an accusation, not a document. The papers, the visas, getting anywhere . . . Everybody stops you. "Oh, you're Syrian?" It's a burden.

A lot of Tunisian youth also want to leave. They have a concept of migration called *harqa*. It means to burn something. People burn their passports. Sometimes they burn their fingertips so that authorities can't take their fingerprints. Then they cross the sea by boat to France or Italy and don't come back.

My friends always used to say, "You've become Tunisian." I remember telling them once, "Yes, I've become so Tunisian that I've reached the point where I want to leave Tunisia." I am so Tunisian that I want to migrate. I'm Tunisian to the point of *harqa*. That's the most Tunisian thing you can do.

Masri

TOKYO, JAPAN

hen we got to Lebanon, I had a lot of depression, especially watching the news from Syria. Assad was gaining control of all the areas. Some rebels were joining terrorist groups and civilians were lost in between. I felt very sad, very lost. You know, survivor's guilt. When you're living inside the siege, all you think about is survival. But when you survive, you start to reflect. You start feeling the pain that you had ignored and denied. I lost my faith in everything. I had existential questions. What is God's plan? All sorts of ideas come to your mind, even suicidal ones. We hadn't escaped hell for heaven. We were still in hell, but a different one.

We moved from north Lebanon to the Bekaa Valley, very close to Syria. You could literally hear mortar shells and bombing on the other side of the border. I joined a Syrian-led NGO in Lebanon. This was a turning point in my life. I was promoted very quickly and became the education program manager. We brought new blood into the traditional way of education. We welcomed volunteers from all over the world. If I convinced my team of something, we could do it. I was able to make change.

I started enrolling in courses online and offline. I learned about the importance of education to help people overcome problems after war. I applied these ideas in our program, developing a neutral curriculum that didn't teach religion or nationalism. Then I found a scholarship sponsored by the Japanese government to get a master's degree in

Japan. My interest was integrating peacebuilding and education. This doesn't just mean education about peace; it means making peace part of the educational system. It's like what Japan did after World War II. They didn't forget the past or focus on revenge. They focused on the future. I don't know if it's possible, but my aim is to do something similar in Syria: to make school a place that is safe for everyone.

THERE ARE about eight hundred Syrians here in Japan. More than one hundred of us are students or their spouses and kids. We were all refugees in Lebanon and Jordan and took this opportunity hoping it could lead to some economic and legal stability. We all came with a lot of motivation. Our university programs are in English, but we were ready to learn Japanese and get adjusted to Japanese society. We had this image of Japan as a very developed country: efficient, powerful, trustworthy. We thought that if we worked hard, we would make the best lives. After all, it's Japan!

The reality we discovered is much more complicated than we expected. The scholarship refers to us as refugees, so we thought that the government was resettling as refugees. It turned out that we just have student visas. After you graduate, you're like any other foreigner in Japan. You need a job to survive, and it's impossible to find good work if you're not fluent in Japanese, which is really hard to pick up on your own. So most Syrian graduates end up getting low-end jobs, like at clothing stores or caring for the elderly. People barely earn the income they need to get by, and a lot of people have to borrow to cover their bills or pay for language school. I know a guy who even had to borrow money from his parents in Syria.

The culture is very different here. It's difficult to make friends. We Syrians are very emotional. We hug and shake hands and invite people over to visit. We open up about everything. In Japan, it's the opposite. People are kind, but distant. It's very formal. Everyone is absorbed with work, at least here in Tokyo. Most neighbors don't respond when you greet them.

Our lives remain unstable. A lot of Syrians in Japan are depressed. Most Syrians would leave if they could, but there's nowhere else we can go. Like many other Syrian families here, my family can't get visas to resettle somewhere else. And Syrians can't even return to Jordan or Lebanon, because they had to give up their UN refugee status when they moved here.

My kids were born in Lebanon. They're now five and three. My daughter loves Japan. She learned a lot of Japanese in kindergarten, so she teaches me. At first, she wanted to go back to her friends in Lebanon. But now she's comparing. Japan has parks and playgrounds; in Lebanon, there's nothing like that. Japan is peaceful. Everything is nice. It's safe and convenient. It's just not the utopia we hoped it would be. I feel like a bird in a gilded cage.

○

WE WANT our kids to have a place to belong to. For me, belonging is not easy to pin down. I used to think that I belonged to my hometown. All of the people I knew used to be in that one place. But now they— that is, the ones who survived—are everywhere. My closest friends are in Germany or Sweden or Canada. My brother is in Turkey, my sister is in Lebanon, my other brother is in Canada, and my other sister is still in Syria. My father and mother are in Syria, and my father-in-law and mother-in-law are in Germany and Turkey. And we are in Japan.

During all those years I spent in Syria, I was always expecting to be killed. If not today, then maybe tomorrow. During the uprising, I moved houses twenty-seven times. For ten years, I was just on the move, on the move, on the move. Now I don't feel connected to any house at all. Not to a country, to a city, or any place. So, you can imagine what home means to me. It means nothing.

For me, a good home is a place that doesn't get bombed or shelled by warplanes. It's that simple. It doesn't matter if it's cold or hot, small or big. It's any place where you can sleep without waking up to an explosion in the middle of the night, wondering if you're wounded or not. I just want somewhere my wife and kids feel comfortable. A place where hopefully, at some point, we can get passports that can help us move around. A place where you can work and not be threatened by the government or any group. A place where we don't feel too much racism. We're okay with a little racism.

I don't feel attached to any physical thing. For me, belonging is to persons, not to places. Maybe I feel attached to some ideas. Like the idea of detainees, of freedom, of fighting dictatorship and extremism at the same time. Now, it's the case of refugees that is my biggest concern. I'm attached to the idea of people who got displaced like me. Refugee rights is fighting dictatorship in a different way.

After we arrived in Japan, I realized that "refugee" is not a good word here. In Japanese, it means a beggar. Like someone who lives on the street and doesn't have a house. Someone who steals or knocks on doors to ask for money. Even UNHCR portrays refugees as miserable and suffering so they can get people to make donations. That's part of the problem. They don't focus on refugees' talent and potential. I want to change this.

Here I've given talks to raise awareness about Syria. In one seminar, I didn't start from 2011. I started with 40,000 BC. *That* is Syria. We talked about culture, food, traditions, celebrations, festivals, architecture, cities. I showed pictures and kept saying, "This is Syria. This is Syria. This is Syria . . . And now this is Syria after the war." I've done more than ten presentations so far, including one to a huge company in Tokyo. I say, "If you're a company and you hire a refugee, that's not charity. If they're good, hire them. If not, don't." I say, "People don't choose to be refugees. They risked their lives to escape to another place, even if it's not as comfortable as their original place." I say, "We're not beggars. We are people who are taken from a whole community and scattered."

Okba

TROGEN, GERMANY

A few days after we tried to go to the church, Haytham and I were coming back from buying groceries in another town. We saw two people walking toward us. They looked like they might be in their sixties. I told Haytham, "Don't greet them." I knew that they weren't going to answer, and that would be really painful.

And then the man said, "Hello."

I was really surprised. I looked around and there was nobody on the street except a cat, and of course he wasn't talking to a cat.

"Are you speaking with us?"

"*Ja.*"

After maybe two months, this was the first person in Germany who greeted me. His name was Ernst, and he was very friendly. I told him, "I'm trying to contact people, but it's hard." I explained that I went to the church but couldn't find Father Amarell." He said, "I know him personally and will talk to him."

That Sunday, Ernst called and said that Father Amarell would be at the church waiting for me. Haytham and I went. I entered with the people and sat in a seat, trying to do the same as the others.

Before they started, Father Amarell came to me and said, "When we finish, I'll give you the microphone. You can tell the community about yourself."

When the prayer finished. Father Amarell said, "Today we have two guests from Syria." Then he gave me the microphone.

Everyone was looking at me. I took the microphone and said, "Hello." The lady translated, "*Hallo.*" Everyone laughed.

Then I started to speak. I was emotional and said, "Thank you so much. There is a place for us here in Trogen. Thank you to the church because you are receiving us right now and helping everyone regardless of religion, color, or background."

That was really from my heart. But after that, I started to lie a bit. I said, "A big thank you to the citizens of Trogen because you are very friendly with us. Whenever I see someone in the street and you smile at us, it means a lot."

Everyone was really pleased with this speech. And strangely, even though everyone before was only speaking German, now they all started to speak English! They said, "Bravo, Okba, Bravo!" I got ten visit cards from different people. One said, "We play volleyball every Wednesday, we can play together." Others said, "We can play football" or "We can get together."

There is a small community center that belongs to the church, and Haytham and I started to go every day. Sometimes we helped with maintenance, like painting or moving furniture. We all worked together to make a beach volleyball court. We worked there for about two months. Every day I met new people. And everyone was friendly. Not like what I thought in the beginning.

THE LADY who translated at the church told me that she had a friend named Miss Kern, an old lady in a nearby village called Feilitzsch. Miss Kern's husband had died two weeks earlier. She was alone and her daughter Angie was moving in with her. Angie was going to bring her furniture and the old lady already had furniture, so they needed to get rid of some.

The translator said, "Maybe you can get some furniture for when you have an apartment."

This was a bit painful for me. It felt like begging. At the same time, I didn't want to say no and look arrogant. I said, "Okay, let's see."

Haytham and I went to Feilitzsch. I saw the old lady and she looked very sad. She gave me a table and a wardrobe and said that she'd leave them in the garage for when I was ready for them. Out of respect, I asked, "Miss Kern, is there anything I can help you with?"

The translator translated. The old lady answered in German, "No, I don't need any help."

In our culture, we don't ask once. We ask two or three times. You insist, or else we don't think you're serious. I tried again. "Are you sure?"

She replied that she didn't need any help. But if she did later, she'd have the translator let us know.

◎

ONE WEEK later, I got a phone call from the translator. "Miss Kern needs help now."

I said, "Gladly!"

I was very happy. Haytham and I went. There was a lot of furniture for us to move. She also wanted us to paint one of the rooms. We had to sandpaper the wallpaper, so it was a lot of work. Evening came and we still hadn't finished.

I said, "Okay, we'll come tomorrow to continue."

Then the old lady moved her hand to give us something: fifty euros.

I was shocked. I'm helping. I'm happy. I feel proud of myself. This is the first time that a German is receiving me in her home. And now that person is offering money!

The old lady insisted. I said, "We would be very glad to come tomorrow. But if you want me to return, please don't give us money. If I take money, I'll be too embarrassed to come back."

She replied, "Okay, don't take money, but I will cook for you. You will eat here."

I said, "Gladly!"

◎

WE WORKED the whole next day and she cooked for us. And then we started to come every day. The old lady started to come and collect us in her car. She spoke only German. I speak Arabic and English. Haytham speaks only Arabic and sometimes even I don't understand his dialect. Haytham would just go to her and speak in Arabic. She didn't understand and would look to me for translation. I'd translate everything in English, but she didn't understand that either. She'd answer in German. We used hands and legs and faces, and she'd laugh a lot.

One time she told us something like, "*Bitte die Möbel auf die Straße bringen.*" Then she went to visit the neighbors. I used voice translation on Google, and it said, "Please put the furniture outside." I thought maybe she wanted to throw it away. So, we took everything out to the street. We worked very fast to show her that we're good workers.

She came back, saw that the living room was empty, and shouted, "What are you doing?" I didn't understand. She said, "*Die Terrasse! Nicht die Straße!*" She wanted to put it in the veranda, not the street. But she wasn't angry. She was shouting and laughing at the same time. It wasn't actually that funny because we had to bring everything back in. But we were laughing the whole time too.

We came every day for two weeks. On the last day, we were having dinner. The old lady spoke in German. Her daughter Angie was there and translated. She said, "Now the work is finished. But this doesn't mean that you don't visit me anymore." She said in German, "From this moment, I am your German grandmother."

I didn't understand in the beginning. She said again pointing to herself, "*Oma.* Granny." I thought, "Okay, this is just an emotional moment. We probably won't see each other again."

But no. Every weekend after that, she'd come for us in her car and drive us to Feilitzsch. We'd make something to eat and sit together.

WHEN YOU get your residency permit, you take your German language course, and the Job Center pays your rent. But how could I find an apartment when I still couldn't speak German? The people I'd met in Trogen helped. Without them, I wouldn't have been able to do it. They called around to find an apartment. They helped transport the furniture.

I got an apartment, but I was a little sad because it was in another town called Hof. It's not far from Trogen, but now I'd only see people to play volleyball on Wednesday or maybe for some activities on weekends. Sometimes I'd go to the church on Sunday just to have the chance to talk with people afterward. Everyone knew me and I didn't feel like a foreigner in the village anymore.

Otherwise, things were boring. I'd go to German class in the morning, finish at one o'clock, and go back home. I had nothing else to do. Near our German school there was an elderly home. Haytham and I decided to go there and volunteer. In the beginning, some people were very distant. Like Frau Hemflig. She was ninety-one years old and had no relatives. Nobody visited her. At first when I brought her food, she'd refuse. Then I started to come to her, and she would talk to me. I didn't understand, but I'd listen and smile. I'd do this so she would smile back. After a few months, we had a good relationship. When I brought her food, she'd smile and take it.

Sometimes we'd wheel people outside to see the town. A lot of times we'd play games. They taught me so many games, but I learned that my job was actually to lose. It was a very easy job. When I lose, they're happy, I'm happy, and everyone is happy.

I ARRANGED to marry my fiancée, Siba, in Syria through my father, who I gave authority to do things in Syria in my name. After a while, Siba got her visa and came to Germany. On her third day, I took her to the elderly home, and she started to do volunteer work with me.

I started a job for a company in Germany. It's a vocational training center and I worked in the international division for development projects in other countries. I traveled to Lebanon to do trainings with refugees there. It wasn't easy for Siba because she'd only been in Germany a few months. When I would travel for two weeks, Oma would come and drive Siba back to Feilitzsch to stay with her. That is something that only real family would do. It meant a lot to me. Oma also bought a mobile phone and installed WhatsApp so she could contact me when I'm abroad. Now we have a WhatsApp group with Siba, Oma, Angie, and me.

The first time I traveled for work I sent nine postcards to the ladies in the elderly home. Until now, when I visit, I see that many of them still have that postcard on their tables by the door.

◎

Do you remember the man I told you about, the one who was the first to greet me in Trogen? Ernst. We talk on the phone every two or three days. We do a lot of activities together. I help him with his computer, and he helps me with other things. I consult with him, and he is like a real father for us. And because of us, he got to know Oma, so sometimes they visit each other too.

Ernst is the head of the Social Democratic Party in Trogen. And through him, I joined the party. You can be a normal member or an active member. I wanted to be an active member. I pay five euros a month and participate in all the meetings. I also feel a little part of that community too. Once, we were in a meeting and they asked why I joined. I joked that I have a lot of political party experience. In Syria, you have to join the Baath party when you're in the fifth grade.

Ahlam

IDLIB, SYRIA

We were sleeping and then, suddenly, the whole house was shaking. We felt the ground shaking too. There was a very loud sound and we couldn't tell if it was shelling or thunder. Then we realized it was an earthquake.

We ran out of the house, barefoot. Everyone was out in the street, shivering and crying. It was raining and freezing cold. We didn't dare go back indoors. We slept in our car for six days. Every now and then there would be an aftershock. We'd get scared all over again. I felt extreme terror. My whole body was shaking, and my throat was dry. It was very strange; I'd never felt that before. Friends died. Relatives died. Entire families died. Ambulances were all over the place. There was a huge number of funerals. We ran out of shrouds or places to bury the dead. We had to bury entire families together in mass graves.

The difference between life and death was less than a second. It was the blink of an eye. There was a family who rushed down the stairs of their building. When they reached the ground floor, they realized that the door was locked from the inside. The father and oldest brother went back up to fetch the key. Then the building collapsed and they died. The rest of the family survived.

The civil defense teams worked day and night. Days after the earthquake, they extracted survivors and saved lives. One woman gave birth underneath the rubble. The mother died but the baby survived. The tools we had for removing the rubble were extremely elementary. If we'd had better equipment, we might have been able to save more lives. Sometimes we didn't even have enough diesel to operate the machinery. We'd collect donations from each other to buy more.

Some Syrians who died in Turkey were sent back to be buried in Syria. Some children came back from Turkey alone. They didn't know whether their parents were alive or dead, and they didn't know who their relatives are. There were children who lost their ability to speak. Others had crush injuries because buildings collapsed on their legs.

Sadness and darkness settled over the whole country. The earthquake was destructive in every sense of the word: spiritually, economically... Syria was already exhausted after twelve years of war, displacement, and death. The country's infrastructure was weak due to all the bombing and shelling. Homes that had been rebuilt after the bombing didn't follow any proper construction standards. There wasn't money for that.

And now, people were out in the streets, homeless again. Families lost all their possessions. They lost their shops, their jobs, their bread-winners themselves. Some people moved in with relatives or rented houses. Others went to shelters erected between the olive trees. Some stayed in shelters just a month or so, and some remain there until today. Living conditions are terrible. Summer is extremely hot and the tents are made of nylon. Some children got heatstroke. The area is filled with dust and insects. Food is scarce. Water is scarce. And when water is available, it's never enough.

☉

MY FEELINGS are like everyone else's. Sadness. Fear. Anxiety. Instability. Not knowing what tomorrow will bring. We're still refugees, after all. We're not in our hometowns. We're not where we come from.

I've been displaced. I lost my brother and father and many relatives. My brother-in-law died in shelling, my nephew's legs were amputated. We've lived all of this hardship, and then the earthquake came and finished us off. For two months afterward, we felt the earth moving beneath our feet and got dizzy.

But I'm still holding on. I still have hope. Sometimes I see despair in children's eyes. I tell them, "It's you who we need to depend on now. Syria needs strong young men and women. We need thinkers. We need innovators." We can't fall into despair. Our country needs us. Kids need an education. Women need assistance. Men need to be made aware. Plants need to be watered. The land needs to be worked. The country needs to be rebuilt.

I belong to my country, my homeland, my people. That's what makes me stay. If I left Syria, I might make a better life. But I belong to this land, my homeland. We all need our close bonds. We need the environment where we have our customs, traditions, culture. This is homeland. You can't live in a country—eat its food, breathe its air, drink its water, deal with its people—and not stand by its side and hold out a helping hand. The stronger our relationships with each other—the more loving and humane—then the more prosperous the homeland will become. There's this saying, "Wherever God plants you, you must bloom." Bloom and produce sweet fruit.

I carry a large burden. But despite everything, I have a garden full of flowers. I have friends. The weather is very nice this time of night. I try to find hope in the simplest of things. I'm still in my homeland, like a tree deeply rooted in the earth. Life goes on, whether we like it or not. So why not have it continue with beauty? Why not have it continue with love, with peace, with a kind spirit? Whether we're upset or cry, whether we lock ourselves up and isolate ourselves . . . Time always passes and this time will pass too. Let it pass with a generous deed, a mark of goodness that remains after you're gone. Many have died, but their legacies continue. Let us be one of those who also leave a good mark.

Rifaie

GAZIANTEP, TURKEY

It's a cliché, but it still feels unreal. A lot of the details are blurred, but what I remember most is the terror.

It was like traumatic experiences that I'd had in Syria. For the longest time, I resisted describing these memories as traumatic because of negative perceptions of people from a refugee background: that they are so vulnerable that you have to tiptoe on eggshells not to disturb them. I don't want to be associated with all that. But even when you don't identify with the term "trauma," it can be there.

When the earthquake happened, I knew it was traumatic. It was the longest one and a half minutes of my life. It was so violent that the word "earthquake" didn't even occur to me. For a long time after that, whenever I sat down, I felt the whole world moving. But I'll tell you something funny: our baby slept through the whole thing.

◎

OUTSIDE, THE scene was postapocalyptic, like doomsday. People looked like zombies. It was snowing and huge crowds were cuddled together. Some people were in their cars. Others went to the parks and burned tires or garbage or whatever they could for heat. I remember that smell.

People were outside in the cold for weeks. In our immediate neighborhood, buildings had huge cracks, but none collapsed. If you walked like ten minutes, then you started seeing serious destruction. I made the argument that, if our building was still standing after two earthquakes, it was relatively safe. Did we want to go to the park and freeze to death? I argued that we should go back inside.

After the initial shock and danger came the photos from other neighborhoods and towns. There were horrific videos of pulling people from under the rubble. My sister wouldn't stop watching them and kept being terrified. I would say, "Stop!" Maybe that was me being in denial of the situation.

Then other consequences set in. The rhetoric against Syrians increased. Most Turks left Gaziantep to stay at their farms or with relatives in other cities. Most Syrians had nowhere else to go, so they stayed in the city. That was portrayed as, "Look, Syrians took over Gaziantep!" Some restaurants were giving out soup to people. Some Syrians were standing in line and some Turkish people said racist things against them. My sister saw some of her Turkish friends posting things on social media like, "It's time for Syrians to go back. We've had enough." It all became unbearable.

©

AROUND THAT time Australian officials were being asked, "What are you doing in response to the earthquake?" Their official response was that they were prioritizing: first, people who had already submitted resettlement applications; second, women and children; third, people registered with UNHCR. My mom and sister ticked all the boxes.

When my wife and I left Australia, we'd given up on resettling them. But after the earthquake, everything changed. We contacted the embassy and they said that they were sending our application to Australia for review. People from all over Australia were contacting me to see how I was doing. They kept telling me, "This is your chance." They started contacting their members of Parliament and the Immigration Department on our behalf. Friends, colleagues, people I barely even knew—they checked in on me and lobbied for my family and me. It showed how many relationships and how much support we have in Australia.

Meanwhile, there were so many decisions that we needed to make. The application could take one month or four months. To do the required health checks we needed to go to Ankara. Should we go to Ankara and then return to a disaster zone? Or do we leave everything in Gaziantep and become homeless? How are we going to survive? Where will we stay? In the end, we decided to leave Gaziantep and not come back. You can imagine how hard it was for my mom to pack into one suitcase all of her life from the past ten years. She said, half-jokingly, "And I had finally just bought those couches!"

We got to Ankara and did health checks. Then we went to Istanbul, where we had friends to stay with. And after that: waiting. Just waiting. The waiting was very, very, very hard. The immigration process triggered so much fear in me. What if something I wrote on the application got misconstrued? What if we weren't clear enough? In one of the earlier applications, I wrote a date wrong. How could I have done that? How could I make a spelling mistake?

My mind was going crazy. This was the single most important event in my life when it came to migration. It couldn't get worse than the earthquake: either my mom and sister got out now or they never would. It was terrifying to think of the alternative. Terrifying, crippling. If the application wasn't approved, I wouldn't leave them in Turkey. But I also couldn't stay in Turkey, because my visa was for three months and it was going to expire.

I was high-strung and overwhelmed. My wife said that, in the five years she'd known me, she'd never seen me so stressed. I think I'm still kind of recovering from that experience. It wasn't just the earthquake and the destruction. The waiting and the dealing with the whole process were traumatic too.

And then I got the phone call from the embassy. The staff member said, "I have some happy news." My mom kissed me on the cheeks and my sister was shouting in the background. Later, we got the email that their travel documents were ready. I booked our flights that day.

◎

ONE OF the beautiful things that came out of this experience is the sense that I have people in Australia. I've got a community here behind me. Sometimes you feel alienated here because of racism or Islamophobia. No place is ideal, but things might not be what they seem on the surface. When the earthquake happened, I realized that I didn't want to go anywhere except Australia. This is where I have citizenship and rights. I have a government and a whole country looking after me.

I often say, "It took an earthquake to get us here." To get resettled, it shouldn't have to get to the point that you're homeless or lose family members. We can criticize the Australian immigration system: the need to increase the humanitarian intake, the inhumane treatment of people arriving by boat ... So many things are wrong. But the speed with which they acted on our case shows that the system works, at least in some way.

I have newfound appreciation now. I started developing a sense of belonging. Before, I didn't feel settled because my mom and sister weren't here. Now that they are, it's all come together. Before, I'd only felt Australian in the technical and legal sense. The earthquake showed me that being Australian is more than that. It's a safety net, a support network, people I can rely on. It's having a country that tries to help.

◎

THE OTHER day, my mom was talking to a friend in Turkey and she said, "Remember how Rifaie always used to call from Australia and say '*Inshallah*, Mama, you'll come here one day'?" My mom told me that the way I said it made her feel that I was sure it would happen. And that used to fill her with hope.

I was so surprised. At that time, I was saying those words without even thinking. I wished that she would come, of course, but I wasn't actually optimistic after the first application was rejected. I guess a mother can sense something more. A mother always knows.

When people hear these stories, they think it's all "Happily ever after." Like every day you wake up feeling happy and grateful. But even to this day, I have this irrational fear that my mom and sister might get sent back. And then there's still the regular struggles of life. Day-to-day stuff, like my sister being a teenager and forgetting to do her homework or staying up too late. It's nice to have the normal challenges of a normal family. Things that everyone else can relate to. Things you can tell someone and they say, "I know how that feels." Not "Oh, I can't imagine."

VII

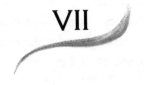

LIVING

MOHAMMED W., MAHA, INSAF,

MAJDY, MEDEA, GHANI, OKBA,

HANI, FATIMA, NOUR

Acclaimed British anthropologist Dame Mary Douglas once posited that home is always a "localizable idea." The question, she reasoned, "Is not 'How?' nor 'Who?' nor 'When?' but 'Where is your home?'" The voices in this book present a different perspective. Even if questions typically focus on the where of home, answers to those questions demand combinations of where, how, who, and when—as well as what and why. Home is a place but also more than a place. It is as complex and multidimensional as life itself.

After journeys in leaving, searching, losing, building, and belonging, people's relationships to home may thus settle into simply living whatever home means for them. Individuals whose journeys unfolded in the preceding pages offer some concluding reflections on their personal experiences of living home or perhaps living without it. Settled in the Netherlands after a long journey via Lebanon, Iraq, Turkey, and Greece, Mohammed W. identifies home with neither where he is from nor where he currently lives, but rather his determination to live without oppression. Like Mohammed W., Maha cannot regard Syria, where her injured son nearly lost his life, as home. She finds belonging in France, however, thanks to the new beginning it gives her family. Maha's daughter Insaf echoes these sentiments. As she moves forward in her quest for home, she carries with her the pain of the thwarted Syrian revolution and her commitment to keeping its dream alive.

Majdy echoes these ideas that connect home to the aspiration to live freely. Having once felt belonging to the apartment that he covered with sticky notes, he now finds that severe restrictions on Syrian refugees make it impossible to find home in Lebanon. Medea speaks of the rising anti-refugee sentiment that is making Turkey similarly inhospitable for displaced Syrians. Nevertheless, Istanbul remains a home for her, as it is where she has grown most as a person. Like Medea, Ghani feels a deep attachment to the country where he has resettled and in which he continues to learn and strive. Now a teacher of barbering, he does not identify with the word "home," but feels a belonging to the values that the United Kingdom represents for him.

For Okba, home remains synonymous with those dearest to him. This includes both his biological family in Syria and his found family in Oma, Angie, and Ernst. Hani offers a contrasting view. Even in the presence of the people he loves most, Chicago cannot substitute for the hometown where his family lived for generations and his own formative years were grounded. In a similar spirit, Fatima continues to yearn for her beloved familial house beside the cemetery in Syria. Her time as a refugee in Jordan, however, has led her to find home in her faith in God. Having turned away from religion, Nour associates home with self-discovery. Because she carries the potential for peace and contentment inside her, she can make home anywhere.

These narratives about living in and after displacement confirm how difficult it is to pin down a single definition of home. Some people associate home with safety, and others link it to freedom, opportunity, or joy. While some tie home to a particular place or set of people, others find home in themselves or in something that transcends the self. Home may be inseparably linked to memories or completely untethered from the past. Understandings of home not only vary across individuals, but also shift across a single individual's lifetime. For many of the speakers in this book, home already means something different from what it did when I recorded their words a few years ago. It will likely continue to change and change again in the years to come.

Home, in other words, is a work perpetually in progress. It is a story written and rewritten throughout our lives. As Hani tells us, it is the details of life that make the story—the precious moments of security, love, authenticity, fulfillment, and belonging that forge our unique bonds to the world around us and to our own sense of self. Attaining these building blocks of home after displacement can demand courage, tenacity, acceptance, and luck; assembling them into something called home requires that one uncovers who one is and what one needs from life. Because it demands work in this way, home is both struggle and achievement. Remembering that encourages us to rejoice with all who have made homes against the odds and offer kindness to those who continue on that path.

Mohammed W.

UTRECHT, NETHERLANDS

Most people confuse belonging and nostalgia. I do feel nostalgic, to be honest. I feel nostalgic for my childhood because it was innocent. I feel nostalgic for the simple lives we used to live.

But I don't want to return to the past. Now if someone said, "Go back to Syria. We'll give you palaces and make you president," I'd say, "Impossible." I would refuse.

The things that I saw did away with feelings of belonging. "Belonging" to me isn't just steel, brick, and the walls of a house. Belonging is tied to what you have been given. And what was I given? I got *qahr*: subjugation and oppression. Subjugation is harder than poverty. *Qahr* is seeing something happen right in front of you, and you don't dare speak out. It creates this feeling, like a mountain on top of your chest. You can call it heartbreak. But it's a particular type of heartbreak. It's heartbreak with anger.

My priorities are needs, not places. Ties to places don't generate any emotions for me. I'm lonely here, but I struggled with loneliness in Syria too. I want to acclimate so I can achieve something. So I can carry on and be happy with myself.

Everything I'm telling you has so much pain and struggle behind it—more than I can put into words. This "home" that you're talking about, I don't think it's here in the Netherlands. And I don't think it's in Syria either. I see home in myself. When I feel content and safe, I will have the greatest home in the world. My home is inside me.

Maha

LE MANS, FRANCE

In France, they distributed refugee arrivals across different cities. We arrived at a house that was ours, where we didn't have to leave. The kids studied and learned quickly. Insaf dealt with all the paperwork for us, and that also helped her learn the language well. For my husband and me, age made learning the language really difficult. After everything that happened to us, my brain was full.

My husband is working now. The boys are in school, the girls are at university. We have enough of everything. We're living dignified lives. We aren't afraid that the police might come, or someone might report us. Freedom and security. Freedom and security. This is the dream.

I'm proud to be Syrian, but I feel that I belong to France. France took us in. We can be a part of this country and we won't be a burden. I hope to be able to give back to the country that accepted us; and if not me, then I'll contribute through my kids. I can give back by respecting this country and its laws. That's belonging.

My sense of belonging to Syria is very complicated. We are hurt and wounded. What Syria can I belong to? The one where I couldn't get medical care for my son? Where my brother was killed? When I dream of Syria, it's a nightmare. Even if Bashar leaves, the system that they created won't just go away. The gang will still be there. And Syria has become an Iranian-Russian colony now, anyway.

Insaf was accepted to one of the best universities in France. I told her, "See, God has made it up to you." But to this day, Insaf still has that fear. She says, "I'm afraid that one day they'll say, 'Go back to your country.'" I tell her that it's impossible. But then again, in Denmark they're sending some families back because they say that Syria is now safe.

We can't forget everything we passed through. To this day we keep in touch with the friends we met when we stayed in Greece. And to this day, I don't get near the ocean.

Insaf

LE MANS, FRANCE

Home is where you can achieve your dreams and ambitions. Home is identity. Home is when you close your door and feel warm. Home is where you're not frightened for your own life or the lives of your loved ones. Where you're not afraid of the future.

I didn't have that feeling in Syria. After what happened in Syria ... after we lost my uncle and my brother got injured and everything else ... it feels like a mirror was broken. You can try to glue the pieces back together, but you'll never bring it back to what it was before.

I'm very proud of being a Syrian who lived every detail of this revolution, from the beginning. I look at my little brother Mahmoud, who is now French more than he is Syrian. He was five when we left Syria and now he's fourteen. His personality developed here. He doesn't know anything about Syria. I want him to know that people in his country did something historic.

Many Syrians say that life before the revolution wasn't that horrible. "We were living," they say. I try to tell them what we were living in Syria was not normal. In forty years of governing Syria, Assad succeeded in making people satisfied with the least of things. Your biggest dream was to get food on the table. I felt like we never saw the sky in Syria because we couldn't look up. Could you speak? No. Could you say that you didn't want to send your kids to the army? No. If you went to a government office, could you say "no" to the employee there? No. If someone decided to report you to the secret police, could you say anything? Could your family search for you? No. You would disappear.

It's not your home when you, as a population, are controlled by a tiny group in power. It's their home, not ours. It wasn't "Syrians' Syria." It was always "Assad's Syria." At school we had big signs saying that slogan, and we were raised on it. Once, when I was in high school, they forced all the students to go downtown to march in a parade in support of the president. I escaped and went home instead. The next day, they called my father and said, "Your daughter wasn't at the parade." He said, "Oh, my, yes. She was sick. She felt very sick." I had to stay home and play sick for three days.

We tried to regain a home, but we couldn't. We tried to get our own Syria, but we couldn't. We held this mirror with a reflection of home and it got shattered in millions of pieces. We got shattered, ourselves. We're broken. All of us.

I'm proud of being Syrian. We're a very multicultural society. We have amazing food and a beautiful, delicate Arabic dialect. But we don't have a homeland. I would love to see Syria in a good situation, at peace. But it will take a lot of time. And by then, it will not be home to anyone.

Now is the time for us to reconstruct our lives and reconstruct them well. I'm no longer afraid of my life being destroyed like it was in Syria. I'm not afraid of anything anymore . . . except maybe that they'll force us to leave. Like my mother says, there's something in me that's not secure. I don't know why. Maybe every refugee or migrant has that feeling, deep inside.

Majdy

BEKAA VALLEY, LEBANON

The Lebanese government issued decisions forbidding Syrians from moving around without a residence permit. The large majority of Syrians here don't have residency permits because they can't afford them. If you're caught without a permit, you get arrested and deported immediately. They don't even give you a week to try to leave Lebanon and go somewhere else. They just hand you over directly to the Syrian authorities.

There are three thing we fear: Lebanese army checkpoints, undercover security officers, and racist civilians who might tell on us. A Lebanese guy wearing civilian clothes might turn out to be with the army or Ministry of Defense. A civilian car might actually be on patrol.

Not long ago, the state sent text messages to all mobile phones in Lebanon stating that there would be legal consequences against any Lebanese person who employed a Syrian who did not have valid residence or who rented an apartment to a Syrian who did not have valid residence. We received those texts too. Some Lebanese people got scared and reported Syrians living near them. A lot of Syrians were deported and turned over to the Syrian regime. Two young men arrested by Lebanese security committed suicide to avoid getting sent to Syrian detention centers and dying there, instead.

My residence permit expired eight years ago, so now I don't leave my house anymore. I haven't left in months, not even to go to the supermarket or take a walk with my wife and daughters. My wife doesn't have a permit, so she doesn't leave the house either. We get everything delivered.

To me, belonging means being in a place where I feel comfortable and where nothing gets in the way of my freedom. That's why I felt a strong sense of belonging to that first house I rented in Lebanon. It was my place. My free space. But today, my house has turned into a curse. You long for your home when you're away from it for a time. When you're away, home is a place to come back to. Now, my house is a prison. The only difference between my house and a prison is that here I can do what I want . . . except leave. A prison is the same: it's a ceiling and walls and a person trapped inside.

☉

WE'RE LIVING in a state of fear here in Lebanon. On top of that, the country is in economic crisis. The currency used to be fifteen hundred Lebanese pounds to the US dollar. Now it's one hundred thousand pounds to the dollar. Lebanon is collapsing as a country, and we Syrians are inside it.

Most Syrians in Lebanon think about leaving any way they can, whether legal or illegal, safe or dangerous. But where can we go? We're not allowed to enter any of the Gulf countries. We're not allowed to enter Egypt or Jordan. We're no longer even allowed to enter Sudan, where there's war.

I've been living in Lebanon for eleven years. I don't want to leave. Two years ago, if someone asked my opinion about migrating illegally to Europe, I would say, "Don't do it! We're living with dignity here. Why risk your life in search of some sort of luxury?" But now, of course I'd take my chances at sea.

A person is nothing but a sum of consecutive hours. I want to offer my time—the most precious thing that I own—to a country that respects me and values me. After what we've been through, I will teach my daughters that a homeland is not where you're born. Homeland is the place that preserves your dignity. Syria isn't my homeland. Lebanon isn't either. I love Syria and I love Lebanon. But I don't feel that I belong to either. I will feel belonging to any country where I'm treated like a human being. A human being. That's it. If Syria ever became a safe country that preserved my dignity and my daughters' dignity, I *might* feel belonging to Syria. I say "might." Not definitely. And not now.

When my daughters grow up, they'll ask me, "Dad, we are Syrian. Why do we live outside Syria?" I will tell them, "We had to leave in order to live." That's why I'm not against any Syrian seeking to migrate by any means possible. Because we Syrians must live. We must live so we can say what happened to us. If no one is left to tell our story, then everything that Syrians have gone through will be lost.

I must live so I can tell my story. I will say that my friend Malek was killed because we chanted "Freedom." We were too young even to understand what freedom means. Now I make my six-year-old memorize the word "freedom." Others said "freedom" and died. Let her say "freedom" and live. And I don't just want her just to say it. I want her to live it. I want her to live freely.

Medea

The most difficult question for any person is, "Who are you?" Now imagine facing that question as a person who is going from one country to another and one struggle to another. Every five or six years, you turn into someone new.

Some people look at this in an ugly way. They don't see the beautiful little details. My experiences have given me this view: you're a little seed that gets to keep growing. Home is where you can be a seed that slowly blooms into a flower. Home is not a single place. It's where you can develop fearlessly and unapologetically. Where you don't have to make excuses for growing up.

If we'd stayed in Syria, there was no way that we would grow. We would be the living dead. When we left Syria and went to Egypt, I didn't shed a tear. In Egypt, I started to experience how to be a seed. When we flew from Egypt to Turkey, I cried my heart out. I hated Istanbul because it took me away from Egypt. Now if I ever had to leave Istanbul, I'd cry two or three times as much. It feels like home, because it's where I have grown so much. More than in Syria or anywhere else in my life.

At the same time, the situation in Turkey is getting difficult. During the last elections, the opposition candidate was promising to make Syrian refugees leave Turkey. He had huge billboards on the highway declaring, "We will kick them out!" It made the whole nation breathe racism, and in a humiliating way. Do you know that American movie where it becomes legal to kill people for one day? It was like that: every

Turkish person seemed to have something against Syrians, and they all started expressing it. Even people I know and invested in all these years. You supported them and they supported you, and now they can't wait to get rid of you?

My closest friends were different. They checked in on us and said, "Don't worry, people are going crazy because of the economic crisis. Things will get better." But the environment made me feel unsafe. It felt like losing part of my home again, but unnecessarily. There was no war, no danger. Why do we need to lose each other and lose home again?

Now my Syrian friends without Turkish citizenship always have in the back of their minds: "Will I get deported? Will it be today or another day? Where should I go next?" These are good people! They have lives in Istanbul. They work here, their families are here. They don't want to leave. But now they are always thinking of Plan B.

If Syrians don't have citizenship in some other country, they have nothing. Just try to imagine how hard it is to be a nation with no government to protect you or your rights. No one has our back. We're orphans. It feels like you're a child who has a mean stepmother, and she keeps pushing you away and you don't know why. The stepmother gives you the nutrition you need to grow up, so you keep running to her. But if she stops feeding you, you'll leave. You'll do what you need to do to live.

For me, Istanbul still feels like home. As long as it gives me opportunities to grow, it will continue to feel like home. But it's getting harder.

Ghani

HUDDERSFIELD, UNITED KINGDOM

What is home? This is the hardest question I've ever had. Maybe I don't have a feeling of home because I've lost my home and become homeless several times. "Belonging" is a better word than "home." I remembered that I answered your question about belonging before and I said that I belong to the UK. I think that I was being small-minded at that time. Now my thinking is broader. My belonging is not to the British people, but to British values. As part of my education, I studied that British values are human values about treating each other fairly and equally. So, now I would say that my belonging is to humanity. That is what this country taught me.

⊙

ONCE ONE of my mates asked me, "What is your goal in life?" I don't like the idea of making goals because, if I achieve that goal, I'll feel that it's the end. I prefer for people to ask me about my next step. It's like stairs. I will keep going.

That's what inspired me to text you again and say, "I have something to add to my story." I thought that it would be good to say that hard times can make us stronger. COVID was a difficult time for me. All the shops were empty, and no one socialized. People avoided each other. Those days took me back to the war. I thought, "How many times will I have to face this?"

I had to close my barber shop because I couldn't afford the rent. I was looking for new work and thought, "Why don't I apply to teach at the college where I was a student?" I had my certificate to teach barbering, so I applied for a job and got it. When I started my journey at this college as a student, I didn't even know how to write my name in English. Now, I'm teaching barbering in English. My former teacher is my colleague.

I have two groups of students: an English group and an English-as-a-second-language group. I have Kurdish students, Arab students, Ukrainian students . . . They all come to learn about hair and beauty. We teach them the terminology and build their confidence. In Arabic, we have a saying: "Don't give me fish, help me to be a fisher." That's exactly what I'm doing.

I also started volunteering for an asylum-seekers' organization. During COVID, I volunteered in a doctor's office as an interpreter. I would go to Arabic-speaking patients and ask what they needed and explain to them about the vaccine. I won an award from the mayor that named me as a refugee ambassador. Refugee ambassadors connect refugees to organizations, and organizations connect us to the government.

I proposed to the organization that they send me refugees and asylum-seekers so they can get a free haircut from my students. It's a win-win. We offer free haircuts to clients who can't afford them. And my students practice and learn.

⟨෧⟩

AFTER BREXIT, the media was always saying, "We don't need refugees. Blah, blah, blah." Government after government makes things harder for us. I say, "Listen. We're a fact. We're not here to beg for benefits or sympathy. We're here to be a part of the community."

I've donated blood twelve times in this country. I'm in good health, so why not support others? Each time somebody receives my blood, I receive a text message. I don't know who that person is, or his religion or race or background. I just know that I helped save somebody's life. My blood type is B+. Whenever I start to get down, I look at myself and say, "Ghani, your blood is 'B positive.' Be positive."

In Syria I went to prison for no reason, but life paid me back. I've been homeless, but life paid me back. Now I'm teaching and working and even starting uni. Every day we learn and grow. We change. So, when you finish my story, don't put a full stop. A full stop means that's the end of my journey. Please don't do that. Instead, put three dots. Like, "To be continued." Maybe I'll call you in two or three years' time and say, "Guess what? I've done this or that." Maybe I will . . .

Okba

I was lucky. That "hello" from Ernst changed my whole life. Without Ernst, I wouldn't know Father Amarell. Without Father Amarell, I wouldn't know the translator. I wouldn't know Oma. I wouldn't have found my apartment. I wouldn't have the elderly home. I wouldn't work for the company I work for now. Everything is connected.

I feel like here is home . . . but not completely home. Something is missing because my parents are in Syria. But Oma is here. Ernst is here. Without my family, I cannot say that I feel at home in Germany. But if I went back to Syria, I would not be one hundred percent happy either. I'd be away from Oma and from Ernst. They're not *like* family. They *are* family for us. And we are the same for them. Not long ago, Father Amarell told me, "Miss Kern said that she's grateful that God sent her two grandsons from Syria after she lost her husband." For this lady, I'm ready to do anything.

Hani

CHICAGO, USA

T hey say home is where the heart is. I don't believe that. Maybe for some people, the two go together. But they don't necessarily go together for me. My heart is with my wife and my kid. My wife is from here. My daughter was born here. I love them. They're the best thing that ever happened to me. But does that mean it's home?

It could mean home in the future. But it doesn't now. You can't just decide overnight, "I'm going to make it feel like home." Home is the details that you don't think about until you lose them. The details that I lived with my whole life. Friends I can swear by. People who will always be there for me because we grew up together. We played soccer in the street together. Everyone came and watched the World Cup at our house because no one else had cable. The first PlayStation on the block was mine, so everybody came and played.

My elementary school. My high school. My seat in the library at college. Our bar in Damascus, Bab Sharqi, which was the best place ever. The store on the corner, where the guy gives me something and I pay him tomorrow because he knows who I am.

Have you heard of al-Fotuwa? Our soccer team. It meant so much to us. We'd go to the stadium four hours before the game because it was so much fun. Al-Fotuwa wins, and it's the best day ever. Al-Fotuwa loses, and everybody is talking about what should they have done differently.

When I think about home, I immediately go to the river. I think anybody from Deir ez-Zor would do that. Everything is built around the river, and it was basically the highlight of the city. I used to go sit by the river when I escaped from high school. My friends and I would play cards the whole day. In summer, we swam every day. We'd grill and camp. At night, there is a bird that makes this noise. I remember that sound in my ear, even now.

All of these details. This is what makes it feel like home. They happened because of everything around them. Because of the community that we lived in. These details . . . you can't create them. They create themselves. You can try to replicate the situation, but it won't have that original feeling. It's like if you went out and said, "I want to fall in love with a girl." It's never going to happen. It happens by itself. Home happens like that. Details create themselves. Suddenly, you have that feeling: "I'm here."

Finding home is also about reconciling with the past. If I learned one thing through everything that has happened, it's to keep moving forward. I moved to Turkey with no money. I didn't know anybody. I didn't have any support system. I said, "I'm going to find myself a job." And I did. I lost a lot of friends in those two and a half years in Turkey. I was working in the camps in Syria and everybody around me was dying. I'd cross the border into Syria and look for the section leader who was managing the tents, and they'd tell me that he died yesterday.

Now, I'm in Chicago. People aren't dying all around me anymore. I try to find something that I can relate to. Back home, I went to the river. Here I go to the lake. Okay, Lake Michigan is not the Euphrates. But it's a body of water. So, I go run by the lake. It means something to me. If we barbecue every day in the summer, we'll make memories here too.

Fatima

AMMAN, JORDAN

When I came to Jordan, I couldn't put my hand on what exactly I'd lost. Back in Syria, we didn't even know what home was because it was wherever we looked . . . A photo of my late father. My father's old notebook that I could touch and feel the entire world's wisdom in his handwriting. The tree that my grandmother used to tell us she planted herself. The house that my mother worked long hours to afford. When I was young, she sold my earrings to help build that house. I grew up knowing that my earrings had become part of our home.

During Eid, everyone visited the cemetery and placed myrtle flowers on graves. My sister and I would look at all the people. "This is my teacher." "That is the shop owner." "This guy, did you know that he's in love with my friend?" "That guy, did you know that he has a crush on me?" You knew everyone. You'd see them, and some of them would also be waiting for the chance to see you.

That is home. I bought from the same supermarket from when I was a young girl still unveiled and with uncombed hair, until I became a young lady. The owner would smile and ask me how I was doing. After I came to Jordan, I heard that he died. I cried so much. He was just the owner of the supermarket, but he was also someone who saw me grow up. He was an icon of my neighborhood: part of my history and my memory.

My grandmother's house always used to be full of people, laughter, happiness, and craziness. She hosted these lively gatherings where we couldn't even hear each other over all the noise. Where's all of that now? Syria is in ruins. Nothing is the same. I love something that no longer exists. In Jordan, my grandmother got cancer and moved in with my mother and me. How did we go from that big family to just three people in exile? My grandmother was dying right in front of our eyes, but we couldn't pay for treatment. The doctors even told my aunt that money was better used to treat children.

Home to me is a feeling. It's the corner in the balcony where I used to sit and look at the sky. I memorized the stars and would trace the shape of my signature between them. This is what home was to me. For a long time here in Amman we lived on the ground floor and I couldn't see the stars. I thought, "There's no sky here. Only Syria has stars."

Home is like a bottle of perfume. You're inside it, unaware. When the war began, the bottle shattered. Suddenly you're walking on broken glass. Home is the sea in which you swim. You don't know what exactly makes it home: the fish, the water, the seaweed . . . You're submerged in it and home is all of it. Then someone takes you out and tosses you somewhere else. They say, "Here's some food. Here's some water. Here's a place to stay. Why aren't you happy?"

Organizations try to offer some financial help, and we must be grateful. They don't know that I'm someone who was attached to every single flower in my homeland. No matter what you give me here, I'm not going to be happy. You'll assume that I'm arrogant. But within us there's a sea, and we're drowning in it. Whenever I grab hold of something, it disappears. We can't explain to others what this water means. You can't know unless you get removed from it too.

Who's going to come and ask you what home means to you? Who cares? They look at us and think, "Why are refugees always making a big fuss? They receive assistance. They get better opportunities than we do. And still, nothing pleases them!" I want to tell them, "Just take it all. Take everything." All I want is to sit on my balcony in Syria and visit my father's grave on Eid. That's worth the whole world to me.

In my heart, going back is an option. But in reality, it's not. Even if I did return, my neighbors wouldn't be there anymore. My relatives are scattered in different countries. Some died. Some were killed. Some were arrested. Only God can reunite us.

Before my grandmother died, I used to say to her, "I don't want to die and be buried in this strange land. At least let our dust become part of the soil of the homeland." But my grandmother had reached a level of wisdom and faith that I had not. She said it didn't matter. She died in Jordan and was buried in Jordan. As a refugee, you're treated as someone temporary. But if you die in exile, it is where you are permanently laid to rest.

⊚

EVERY PERSON has a different perspective. Some people, like my brother, blame the revolution for their misfortunes. He says, "We were living fine. Let the regime be rotten. I had a good life." Other people who were revolutionary activists say that they wasted their lives for this thing called the homeland. A relative of mine became paralyzed. He says, "I gave my health for my country. But now there's no country and there's no God too."

For me, all of this has deepened my faith. There was a point when I was depressed. Now I feel that the best thing in life is to be close to God. When I saw my grandmother take her last breath, I thought, "Everything we're crying for in this life means nothing. There's a larger universe, and that should be the home for your soul."

In all this absurdity, there is a hidden mercy. I had a professor who used to say that gold has to be subjected to extremely high temperatures to remove impurities. That's what happened to us to make us understand what really matters. You're here for a reason. And just like you're learning, someone will learn from you. God placed me in this situation of weakness and told me, "Every hardship is followed by ease."* God puts under trial those who He loves the most because He wants them to reach a higher degree of faith.

In Syria, I was a daydreamer. I imagined a perfect life. Marrying the perfect husband, having lovely children, becoming an important trans-

---

* *The Quran*, 94:5.

lator. How attached I used to be to small things! I used to worry about the color of my shoes and the height of my heels. I had trouble throwing away any piece of paper. If a friend signed something for me, I'd keep it as a memento.

I'm not attached to anything anymore. Now we move from one house to another, and there are no feelings involved. God had me go through this harsh experience so I wouldn't get attached to temporary things, but instead to something more heavenly. I don't know what the path is, but I'll put my hands in the hands of God and trust Him.

I used to dream of being pretty and successful. But that's not my world anymore. My home is no longer on land. My home is my God. My home is in the sky. Sometimes I look at the stars that I used to watch in Syria. They are the same here, after all. Stick with the sky. The earth changes, but the sky will guide you. This earthly life is only a corridor. I'm no longer rooted in the earth. I'm rooted in the sky.

Nour

AARHUS, DENMARK

What differentiates home from other places is that you feel like everything is stable. You know your neighbors and your environment. Your family is there. You have an idea of where you're going in life. You have all these memories in that space.

In Syria, my days were stable because I had Grandpa and Grandma, my cousins, my school, and all the privileges that came from my family. At the same time, I remember feeling incomplete. There was something missing. I couldn't be critical. Whether it was about the role of women or my government, my culture, or my country, I was not allowed to say anything. The revolution came at the right time for my generation because a lot of people shared the same frustration.

Home is related to the process of self-discovery. Leaving religion forced me to form my own values. Before, I was trying to go to heaven. Now I ask, "What am I going to do during this lifetime on earth?" The longer I've been away from Syria, the less I'm a "typical Syrian." I'm not sure if that's good or bad, but it's what happens as you grow as a person. I've had to make my own definition of being Syrian. The more in touch I become with myself, the more peaceful and content I become. I didn't have that before. It comes with understanding the bigger picture.

I imagine my life as a puzzle. During my life in Syria, I had the frame. All of the corner pieces were full, and it had some little pieces here and there, but a lot was missing. Moving to Turkey, I filled in some of the pieces. Being in Denmark over the past years, I found the main part. The frame is a constant reminder of where I come from and who I am. Now the picture is becoming clearer, calmer, and more organized. I'm not searching for pieces all over the place. I have the main pieces figured out. I just need to fill in a few empty parts. The puzzle will always be missing something. Sometimes you put a piece in and then you realize it's in the wrong place, so you move it somewhere else. The beautiful thing is that, in the end, the journey makes sense.

⊙

WHEN I first moved to Denmark, I always felt unsettled. Now I realize that home has become my own company. It's myself. Home is literally me, my own body. Wherever I go, I can manage to make it feel like home.

The journey of becoming comfortable with yourself is also reflected in the environment in which you live. As humans, we express ourselves by the way we arrange things in our spaces. We're all different and that's why everyone's homes are different. In five years in Denmark, I've lived in three different cities and six different apartments. I felt like each one was home to me because I started to build my rooms to reflect my personality. My first room at the university felt like home. I thought it was where I belonged, and I was so sad when I had to move. Then, the second apartment was comfortable and nice, and I was also sad to leave. When I look at where I live now, it feels even more like home than the previous places.

The things that make you who you are is what makes a place your home. The biggest thing for me is the childhood photo album that I took with me from Syria. There are photos of the little me who had no idea that someday she would be living on her own in Denmark. With these photos, the little me will always be watching over the older me. In my apartment, I have traditional foods that I bought from the Middle Eastern supermarket. It's a constant reminder that I used to live in Syria, and this is what I ate every day. It's a reminder of being settled and stable there, but now it comes with this bigger, more complete picture of who I am. These things are part of home.

I have this rocking chair like Grandpa had. It reminds me of summer evenings when he would be on his chair, smoking *argila* and listening to us kids. We would laugh loudly and argue about random things, and he would just watch and smile. These are my imprinted childhood ideas about home.

I found this carpet which is like the kind we used to have. Here, people don't really care about carpets. To me, if the floor doesn't have a carpet, is it even a home? You need to step on something soft. Sometimes when I'm listening to a song and feel my feet on the carpet, I have flashbacks of little me running around our house. I have the same sensation of moving between the floor and the carpets and hiding from my brother, or whatever I was doing. Now, sometimes I like to walk barefoot because it brings back those memories of walking between rooms at Grandma's house. It's like this texture transports me in time. In that moment, I'm not a twenty-eight-year-old in Denmark. I'm a six-year-old running after my grandma.

It's comforting. But I also can't help feeling sad. I will probably never get to see that place again. Sometimes I feel like I've forgotten so much about home that if you put me back there now, I would get lost. I have a phobia of forgetting home, so I always look through my photo album. I use it as my reference, so I don't forget. These printed images refresh home in my mind. If one day I wake up and forget how my room or my grandma's house looked, I'll know that I'm losing myself. At that point, I'll know that I'm not in a good place.

My room now feels like home. But I wouldn't call it "home" yet. I think home is somewhere where I won't be alone. Home is where people love you for who you are and don't put rules or conditions on loving you. It's where you can be your authentic self with no propaganda, no pressure, and no judgment. Having a loving environment is what makes a space home. So home is where I can be myself, like I am now, but with people I love. I hope it will happen at one point in my life.

Acknowledgments

I have an unpayable debt to the hundreds of Syrians who selflessly welcomed me into their lives and shared with me their ideas, feelings, and experiences. They taught me the meanings of dignity, commitment, and resilience. Though they are too many to name, I hold each of them in my heart. I am forever changed, and will be forever humbled, by the privilege of having met them.

I am exceptionally grateful to those who went above and beyond in helping me during physical and virtual trips across the Syrian diaspora, as well as in helping me connect with potential interviewees. I give special thanks to Rasha Ajalyaqeen, Sara Ajlyakin, Maha Atassi, Patricia Begley, Tameem Emam, Salah Falyoun, Nour Flyahan, Insaaf Haddad, Ghaidaa al-Haj and family, Lina Omran, Yasmin Marei, Mohammed al-Masri and family, Anne-Marie McManus, Ahmad Khodr Minkara, Moro, Hassan Almossa, Oula Ramadan, Rand, Medea Safadi, Nahed Samour, Alhakam Shaar, Salma al-Shami, Suheib, Rana Sweis, Rosanne Symons, Rifaei Tammas, and Ahmed Yassin. Their generosity is an inspiration, and their trust in me is an honor.

Had I had to transcribe and translate all interviews myself, this book would have taken another decade to finish. Thankfully, I was met with skilled assistance from translators, transcribers, and undergraduate research assistants, including Sumaya Tabbah, Rasha Algohary, Brianna Bilter, Sarah Richman, Zinya Salfiti, Carol Silber, Rohan Subramaniam, and Laila Skramstad. Felix Beilin was not a research assistant as much as a thought partner and critic, and the book is much better for it. Wonderful friends Rana Kazkaz, Andre Bank, Christa Kuntzelman, Carol Silber, and Nada Sneige Fuleihan, read drafts and offered invaluable feedback. Hael Ashoy and Trudi Langendorf contributed to every stage of this project, pulling upon their rich experiences and endless powers of observation to broaden my thinking and offer insightful comments on the written work. I am lucky to have had the chance to learn from them.

This book is one harvest from a larger research project on Syria made possible by support from the Alexander von Humboldt Foundation and Europe in the Middle East–The Middle East in Europe (EUME) at the Forum Transregionale Studien in Berlin, Germany. I am grateful to Georges Khalil, Friederike Pannewick, and the EUME staff for facilitating the immense gift of repeated stays in Germany. I am also thankful for research funding support from the Alumnae of Northwestern University and Northwestern's Weinberg College of Arts and Sciences. This research would not have become the book it is without my agent, Ayesha Pande, and editor, Haley Bracken. I thank them, and Liveright, for believing in me.

Throughout this project, I have been fortunate to count on emotional support from my siblings, Alicia and Charlie Pearlman, and dear friend Jana Lipman. I would have gone crazy a long time ago if not for my partner, Peter Cole, who lived every moment of this book's creation and whose patience, intelligence, and humor kept me going. My father, Michael Pearlman, and grandmother, Margaret Pearlman, both passed away during the years in which I was working on this project. My father instilled in me a passion for researching and writing and taught me the value of humility. My grandmother, who worked for social justice and political change during all of her 102.5 years, taught me more than I can express. This work is inspired by her example as an activist, an artist, and a listener. She will always be home for me.

Chronology

1946 – 1963

1946: Syria gains independence from France. Its parliamentary system is dominated by landed aristocracy and wealthy merchants.

1947: The Baath Party forms as a revolutionary movement committed to Arab unity and socialism. It especially attracts rural youth, religious minorities, and some army personnel.

1948: Approximately 750,000 Palestinian refugees are expelled or forced to flee during the first Arab-Israeli War. About 90,000 settle in Syria.

1949: A military officer overthrows Syria's elected government, the first such coup in the modern Middle East. Continued military interventions in politics, as well as class and ideological conflict, topple seven governments by 1963.

1963 – 2010

1963: Army officers affiliated with the Baath Party seize control of the state, establishing a single-party regime.

1967: In the second Arab-Israeli War, Israel captures Syria's Golan Heights.

1970: General Hafez al-Assad, the Minister of Defense and a Baath regime leader, launches a bloodless coup. During his next thirty years as president, Assad centralizes personal power and builds a strong authoritarian regime and security state.

1976: In the context of the Lebanese civil war, Assad moves Syrian troops into Lebanon where they remain until 2005. The intervention ignites Syrians' discontent with corruption, inflation, and security abuses, prompting opposition activity and regime repression in response.

1982: The Syrian Muslim Brotherhood launches an insurrection in the town of Hama. The Assad regime responds with a scorched-earth assault that leaves up to tens of thousands dead, warning subsequent generations of its capacity for violence.

2000: Hafez al-Assad dies. Pledging reform, his thirty-four-year-old son Bashar assumes the presidency.

2000–2002: During an opening called the "Damascus Spring," civil society activists spearhead petitions and discussion groups calling for greater freedom and rule of law. A government crackdown silences the movement.

2006–2010: Severe drought, combined with government mismanagement of the crisis, compels as many as 1.5 million Syrians to migrate from rural areas.

2011

JANUARY 14: A popular uprising forces Tunisia's authoritarian president to resign, launching what becomes known as the "Arab Spring."

FEBRUARY 17: After police beat a young man in the Damascus Old City, an unprecedented demonstration chants, "the Syrian people will not be humiliated."

MARCH 15: Syrian activists online call for mass demonstrations against the Assad regime. A few hundred protest before police violently disperse crowds and arrest participants.

MARCH 18: After children are arrested for anti-Assad graffiti, thousands gather in the southern city of Daraa for Syria's first large-scale protest. Security forces open fire, killing two. Despite state control of media, news travels across the country.

MARCH 25: With Daraa under siege, tens of thousands protest across Syria. Demonstrations continue, grow, and remain overwhelmingly nonviolent for months. The regime uses beatings, house raids, arrests, torture, and other violence to quash the budding revolution.

APRIL: US president Barack Obama imposes sanctions on Syria. As the Syrian death toll passes 1,000, Canada and the European Union (EU) impose similar restrictions. Regime violence continues to intensify, nonetheless. Obama eventually declares that Assad is illegitimate and should resign.

JULY: Defected military officers establish the opposition "Free Syrian Army." As the uprising militarizes, the regime escalates its crackdown to use of artillery, shelling, cluster bombs, and missiles.

AUGUST: Exiled oppositionists form the Syrian National Council to represent the revolution. Later superseded by the Syrian National Coalition, these leadership bodies struggle to build influence abroad and credibility inside Syria.

2012

JANUARY: Operatives of al-Qaeda, some of whom had earlier entered Syria from Iraq, form al-Nusra Front to fight to replace Assad with an Islamic state. Other armed groups with Islamist ideologies subsequently emerge.

JUNE: In Geneva, the United Nations (UN) convenes the first of what will be years of peace talks between the Syrian government and opposition. They fail to end the conflict.

JULY: Jordan, together with the UN High Commissioner for Refugees (UNHCR), opens the Zaatari refugee camp. Zaatari remains the largest refugee camp in the Middle East and one of the largest in the world.

JULY: Rebel forces launch an offensive to take Aleppo, Syria's largest city and economic capital. The operation stalemates, and the city divides between regime and rebel control.

AUGUST: Syrians in rebel-held territory document remnants of "barrel bombs." These munitions—oil drums, gas tanks, or other containers packed with explosives and shrapnel—become among the war's chief sources of death, destruction, and displacement.

NOVEMBER: The UN High Commissioner for Human Rights submits a report suggesting that crimes against humanity have been committed in Syria. It goes on to submit dozens of reports documenting such crimes.

2013

APRIL: A rift between al-Nusra Front and al-Qaeda results in a new group called the Islamic State of Iraq and Syria (ISIS).

JUNE: After an eighteen-month siege, Hezbollah, Iranian, and Assad forces retake control of the strategically located town al-Qusayr.

AUGUST: The Assad regime launches a chemical attack on rebel-held Eastern Ghouta, killing more than 1,400 people. The United States reaches an agreement with Russia to remove Syria's 1,300-ton chemical weapon stockpile. Still, the Assad regime carries out another 294 chemical weapons attacks by 2018.

SEPTEMBER: UNHCR estimates that more than two million Syrians have become registered refugees, making Syria the world's largest refugee crisis.

2014

JANUARY: Claiming that it can no longer verify information, the UN stops counting deaths in Syria.

JANUARY: Forensic science experts authenticate 55,000 digital images detailing systematic torture, starvation, and murder of detainees in Syrian prisons. The images, smuggled out of Syria by a defected prison officer code-named Caesar, become known as the Caesar photographs.

MAY: Russia and China veto a UN resolution condemning the Syrian government's human rights abuses. By 2023, Russia vetoes eighteen UN resolutions on Syria.

JUNE: From its capital Raqqa in northeast Syria, ISIS launches an offensive into Iraq, captures Mosul, and declares the establishment of the Islamic State (IS). At its peak, IS governs territory encompassing one-third of Syria and 40 percent of Iraq.

SEPTEMBER: The United States leads a coalition of eighty-five countries in a campaign of airstrikes to destroy IS. Its only major military intervention in Syria, the US targets IS and not the Assad regime. To avoid deploying ground troops, the US partners with what coalesces into the Syrian Democratic Forces (SDF), a coalition of Arab and Kurdish fighters led by Kurdish forces. Turkey regards the SDF as terrorists.

OCTOBER: Lebanon asks UNHCR to stop registering new Syrian refugees. In the months to follow, it imposes new restrictions on Syrians' entry.

DECEMBER: By the end of 2014, irregular Mediterranean land and sea crossings to Europe have increased nearly 200 percent from 2013. More than 3,500 migrants have died, making 2014 the deadliest year on record for migration.

2015

MARCH: The UN reports that 6 percent of Syria's population have been killed or injured, some 80 percent live in poverty, and the majority of children no longer attend school. Satellite images show a country "plunged into darkness."

APRIL: As migrant drownings spike, EU leaders declare renewed efforts against migrant trafficking. Smuggling only escalates, however, as it shifts from the Central Mediterranean route between North Africa and Italy toward the shorter Eastern Mediterranean route from Turkey to Greece.

MAY: UNHCR calculates that donor countries have delivered only 23 percent of the funding that they pledged to support assistance to Syrian refugees and host communities in the Middle East. Aid shortfalls exacerbate deteriorating conditions and despair, pushing more refugees to attempt to migrate to Europe.

JUNE: The EU agrees to resettle some refugees from outside the Union and also to resettle some refugees from Italy and Greece to other member states. Resettlement numbers pale before demand, however, and migrant crossings continue.

JULY: Hungary erects border fencing against what observers increasingly call a "refugee crisis." Bulgaria, Macedonia, Slovenia, and Austria soon follow suit.

AUGUST: German Chancellor Angela Merkel suspends for Syrians the Dublin Regulation, which compels asylum seekers to register in the first EU country of entry. The decision spurs more refugees and migrants to attempt to reach Germany.

SEPTEMBER: The Russian Air Force enters the Syrian war in support of the Assad government. By 2019, a reported 45,000 Russian sorties have killed 15,000–25,000 people.

DECEMBER: By the end of 2015, the number of migrants entering Europe via the Mediterranean increases by 350 percent from the previous year. Of the 1.3 million new arrivals applying for asylum, 29 percent—the largest share from any nation—are Syrian.

2016

MARCH: In a deal with the EU, Turkey agrees to halt irregular migration from its shores. Migration increasingly shifts back to the deadlier Central Mediterranean route.

JUNE: After a suicide bombing by IS, Jordan closes its border with Syria. It keeps it largely closed until 2021.

AUGUST: Turkey launches "Operation Euphrates Shield," an invasion of Syrian border regions, to combat both IS and Kurdish forces. After another two major military operations, Turkey occupies about 3,400 square miles of Syria by 2019.

AUGUST: The United States resettles its ten thousandth Syrian refugee. Meanwhile, 4.8 million Syrian refugees are registered in countries in the Middle East.

DECEMBER: With Russian air support and after months of battle, the Syrian government retakes all of Aleppo. The city's population shrinks from three million before the war to about one million during the peak of violence.

2017 – 2023

JANUARY 2017: Russia, Turkey, and Iran hold Syria peace talks in Astana, Kazakhstan, launching an alternative to the stalemated UN-led Geneva talks.

OCTOBER 2017: The SDF takes control of Raqqa. By December, IS has lost 95 percent of its territory.

JANUARY 2017: Newly inaugurated US president Donald Trump issues a ban on entry into the US of nationals from seven majority-Muslim countries, including Syria. He suspends refugee resettlement for 120 days and bans Syrian refugees indefinitely.

JUNE 2018: Turkey finishes erecting a 475-mile wall sealing its border with Syria.

MARCH 2018: Government forces retake Eastern Ghouta after a five-year "surrender or starve" siege cutting off food and medicine. Civilians must choose either to remain under regime control or be displaced to rebel-controlled Idlib province.

OCTOBER 2019: Trump removes the approximately 1,000 US troops stationed in northeast Syria to support the SDF against ISIS. Turkey begins an offensive into Syria, expelling Kurdish fighters from border regions. Abandoned by the United States, Kurdish forces seek help from Assad.

DECEMBER 2019: Syria and Russia launch a major offensive on Idlib province, displacing nearly a million people toward the Turkish border before the Turkish army intervenes and a ceasefire is reached.

APRIL 2020: Exercising the principle of universal jurisdiction, Germany tries two Syrian security officers on charges of crimes against humanity. Syrian asylum-seekers identify the officers, who also arrived in Germany as asylum-seekers, as having tortured them in prison.

JUNE 2020: The "Caesar Syria Civilian Protection Act" expands US sanctions to punish the Syrian government and deter foreign investors from business with the Syrian government.

APRIL 2021: Denmark judges some parts of Syria to be safe and begins reviewing residency permits for more than a thousand Syrian refugees. While many cases of revoked residency are overturned, some Syrians in Denmark move into deportation centers or flee.

MAY 2021: Bashar al-Assad is elected president for a fourth term with a reported 95 percent of the vote.

SEPTEMBER 2022: The Syrian Ministry of Health declares a cholera outbreak, compounding crisis in a healthcare sector in which less than half of hospitals and public health centers function fully.

DECEMBER 2022: The UN estimates that 15.3 million people in Syria—about 70 percent of the population—need humanitarian assistance.

FEBRUARY 2023: Devastating earthquakes strike near the border between Turkey and Syria. Urgent disaster relief is delayed to rebel-held northwest Syria due to the prior blocking of humanitarian corridors by Assad, Russia, and China.

MAY 2023: The Arab League votes to reinstate Syria's membership, marking a turning point in the normalization of the Assad regime.

AUGUST 2023: The Syrian pound, which traded at 47 to the dollar in 2011, hits a record low of 15,500 to the dollar. Spurred by deteriorating economic conditions, protests against the Assad regime erupt in Sweida province and some other parts of Syria.

Notes

Introduction: The New Diaspora

1. United Nations High Commissioner for Refugees (UNHCR), "Syria Regional Refugee Response," last updated April 18, 2024, https://data.unhcr.org/en/situations/syria; Eurostat, *Asylum Applications Database*, https://ec.europa.eu/eurostat/databrowser/view/migr_asyappctza_custom_11097010/default/table?lang=en; UNHCR, "Syria Regional Refugee Response: Durable Solutions," last updated April 18, 2024, https://data2.unhcr.org/en/situations/syria_durable_solutions; UNHCR, "Syria Operational Update (February–March 2024)," April 2024, https://reliefweb.int/report/syrian-arab-republic/syria-operational-update-february-march-2024#:~:text=The%20Syria%20crisis%20entered%20its,tension%20impacting%20relatively%20stable%20areas.

2. Ghassan Hage, "At Home in the Entrails of the West: Multiculturalism, 'Ethnic Food' and Migrant Home-Building." In *Home/world: Space, Community, and Marginality in Sydney's West*, ed. Helen Grace, Ghassan Hage, Lesley Johnson, Julie Langsworth, and Michael Symonds (Annandale: Pluto Press, 1997), 103.

3. Michael Jackson, *At Home in the World* (Durham, NC: Duke University Press, 1995).

4. bell hooks, *Belonging: A Culture of Place* (New York: Routledge, 2009), 1.

5. Yi-Fu Tuan, "Rootedness versus Sense of Place," *Landscape* 24, no. 1 (1980), 5.

6. Edward Said, "Reflections on Exile." In *Reflections on Exile and Other Essays* (Cambridge, MA: Harvard University Press, 2002), 137.

7. M. Murat Erdoğan, "Syrians Barometer: A Framework for Achieving Social Cohesion with Syrians in Türkiye," November 2022, https://www.unhcr.org/tr/wp-content/uploads/sites/14/2023/01/SB-2021-I%CC%87ngilizce-19-Ocak-2023.pdf, 159.

8. UNHCR, "Syria: Eighth Regional Survey on Syrian Refugees' Perceptions and Intentions on Return to Syria," May 2023, https://reporting.unhcr.org/syria-eighth-regional-survey-syrian-refugees%E2%80%99-perceptions-and-intentions-return-syria.

9. UNHCR, "Syria Regional Refugee Response: Durable Solutions," last updated June 30, 2023, https://data2.unhcr.org/en/situations/syria_durable_solutions.

10. Human Rights Watch, *"Our Lives Are Like Death": Syrian Refugee Returns from Lebanon and Jordan*, October 2021, https://www.hrw.org/sites/default/files/media_2021/10/syria1021_web.pdf; United Nations Office of the High Commissioner for

Human Rights, *"We did not fear death but the life there": The Dire Human Rights Situation Facing Syrian Returnees,* February 2024, https://reliefweb.int/report/syrian -arab-republic/we-did-not-fear-death-life-there-dire-human-rights-situation-facing -syrian-returnees-february-2024-enar; Voices for Displaced Syrians and Operations and Policy Center, *Is Syria Safe for Return? Returnees' Perspective,* November 2021, https://voicesforsyrians.org/wp-content/uploads/2021/12/Syrian-Returnees-11.12 .2021.pdf.

Part I: Leaving

1. Al-Jazeera, " 'Bashar Out!': Protests in Southern Syria over Economy Now Target President," September 1, 2023, https://www.aljazeera.com/news/2023/9/1/bashar -out-protests-in-southern-syria-over-economy-now-target-president.
2. United Nations Development Programme-Syria, "Amid Record High Food Insecurity in Crisis-Hit Syria, UNDP and Humanitarian Partners Join Efforts to Increase Access to Affordable Bread for Vulnerable Syrians," June 1, 2022, https://www.undp .org/syria/press-releases/amid-record-high-food-insecurity-crisis-hit-syria-undp -and-humanitarian-partners-join-efforts-increase-access-affordable-bread.

Part II: Leaving, Again

1. United Nations News, "Refugee Resettlement Numbers Fall to Lowest in Two Decades: UNHCR," November 19, 2020, https://news.un.org/en/story/2020/11/ 1078052.

Part III: Searching

1. UNHCR, "Syria Regional Refugee Response," last updated April 18, 2024; https:// data.unhcr.org/en/situations/syria.
2. See Eurostat, *Asylum Applications Database,* https://ec.europa.eu/eurostat/data browser/view/migr_asyappctza_custom_11097010/default/table?lang=en.

Part IV: Losing

1. Leïla Vignal, *War-Torn, The Unmaking of Syria 2011–2021* (London and New-York: Hurst Publishers/Oxford University Press, 2021), 106.

Part V: Building

1. Philip Oltermann, "How Angela Merkel's Great Migrant Gamble Paid Off," *The Guardian*, August 30, 2020, https://www.theguardian.com/world/2020/aug/30/angela-merkel-great-migrant-gamble-paid-off.

2. Mohammed Hardan, "How Syrian Refugees Contributed to Turkish Economy," *Al-Monitor*, May 11, 2021, https://www.al-monitor.com/originals/2021/05/how-syrian-refugees-contributed-turkish-economy; Global Compact on Refugees, "Higher Education for Syrian Youth," https://globalcompactrefugees.org/good-practices/higher-education-syrian-youth.

Part VI: Belonging

1. Linn Miller, "Belonging to Country—A Philosophical Anthropology," *Journal of Australian Studies* 27, no. 76 (2003): 215–23.

2. Andrew Geddes and Adrian Favell, eds., *The Politics of Belonging: Migrants and Minorities in Contemporary Europe* (Aldershot, England, and Brookfield, VT: Ashgate, 1999); Nira Yuval-Davis, "Belonging and the Politics of Belonging," *Patterns of Prejudice* 40, no. 3 (2006): 197–214.

Part VII: Living

1. Mary Douglas, "The Idea of a Home: A Kind of Space," *Social Research* 58, no. 1 (1991), 289.